Renaissance Belle

*The stories in this book reflect the author's recollection of events. Some names, locations, and
identifying characteristics have been changed to protect the privacy of those depicted. Dialogue
has been re-created from memory.*

Made in USA - Kendallville, IN
26073_9781953000262
06.17.2022 1340

A MEMOIR ABOUT LOVE, LOSS AND
FINDING BEAUTY IN EVERY NEW BEGINNING.

Renaissance Belle

JACQUELINE M. SMITH

Dedication

This book is dedicated to the Author of my story. The One who is the very air I breathe.

Thank you, God for your goodness yesterday, today and all my days ahead. You have been present and faithful in every moment of my life. I am forever grateful. It's because of You, Lord that I believe that beauty can be found in ashes. It's because of You, Lord that I look forward to my happily ever after beyond the sky.

David William Smith, my amazing husband who loved me faithfully, generously and creatively every day of our thirty years together. Dave, you were my dream come true and continue to be the love of my life. You taught me to look for God in the details and to embrace every moment because this life is a great adventure. Your faith and example in this life continues to impact others. I know that what lies ahead there doesn't even compare to the wonderful life we shared on this earth. Knowing this separation is only temporal, I look forward to the day we're together again.

My children: my heart, Brittany, David, and Jonathan (Jonny). You have grown up to become amazing adults. You are decent, honest, and loving. You are each gifted and talented in a myriad of ways. Like your father, you are creative artists in many genres. All I have to do is look in your eyes to see your daddy.

When I hear your voices, I hear his. When you hold me in a bear hug, I hear his heartbeat. I am beyond proud of you and the three wonderful humans you have chosen to spend your lives with.

Seth, Heather, and Rachel, thank you for loving my treasures. I love each of you as my own. As of this writing I have two beautiful grand boys, Asa and Ezra and another precious grand baby on the way. They have filled my heart with a unique kind of love I never knew existed. They are my happy!

My mother, Aurora and the rest of my big, beautiful, passionate family. Imagine the food and gatherings we'll continue to enjoy together in eternity! Los amo a todos!

My Smith-side of the family. Thank you for loving me from day one. We are family forever.

My dearest friends who have loved us and believed in us in every season. True friendship is in the laughter and in the tears. You've been there for both. Thank you.

Table of Contents

Dear Reader,

If you are reading this, it means that you have chosen to take a journey with me through some significant parts of my life story. This is not an all-encompassing account, as there is so much more I could have shared and there is so much more yet to be written.

Most of what I share here flowed out of me in the first year after my Dave went to Heaven. Feelings, emotions, tears, memories and love all spilled out from the deepest parts of me unto the pages before you. I will be forever grateful for the love Dave and I still share. Someone once told me that as long as I talk about my husband, he will never die. True words.

I believe everyone has a story and every story is worth sharing.
Thank you for letting me share mine with you.

—Jackie

I'M
HUNGRIER
FOR HEAVEN
THAN
I'VE
EVER
BEEN.

THAT'S
BECAUSE
HALF
OF
ME
IS
ALREADY
THERE.

Introduction

Renaissance Belle means beautiful new beginning.

When you have lived out a real-life love story, you have to tell it. You have to share it. My love story is one of the most beautiful to ever exist and it lives on even after the blow of death. Telling my story is something I feel compelled to do. It's something I feel I was made to do.

My hope is that my story will inspire and encourage. That it will bring hope to someone's life. It might make you smile or shed a tear. Perhaps it will convince you that God is present in our everyday lives. More than anything, my prayer is that it will fill your heart with the truest love of all, God's love. He is the only reason I was fortunate enough to know this kind of once in a lifetime love. A faithful husband's love.

I give HIM, my Creator, all the credit for my story. It's really His story, after all. He wrote it for me before I was even born. I am simply the actor in this story, living it out as it was laid before me, with all its twists and turns, intrigues and surprises. I believe the Writer allowed me, in His Sovereignty, to fill in some blanks along the way with decisions and life choices which made me turn this way or that. But He always knew how the important parts should turn out. He gently guided me as to where my steps should go, especially when I allowed Him to really take the reins.

Now I get to share it with others.

In this latest chapter of my personal story, I find myself at the start of a new journey, surprisingly having to navigate through unexpected, uncharted territory without the love of my life. It's a new beginning I never imagined or wanted. Although I am broken, I am determined to find beauty in ashes and purpose in pain.

We all have a story to tell. Some are more heart-wrenching than others. Some are complicated and dramatic. Some are more simple and sweet. But I have learned that every story is important, significant, and meaningful. I believe that whether happy or sad, and even in the darkest of times, every journey has lessons to offer. There's purpose in each road that's traveled…and there's beauty to be found in every new beginning.

Here's to your Renaissance Belle!

DEATH
CANNOT
STOP
TRUE
LOVE.
ALL
IT
CAN
DO
IS
DELAY
IT
FOR
A
WHILE.

THE PRINCESS BRIDE

November 24, 2017, 3:25 AM

Suddenly and unexpectedly, my world came to a crashing halt. Everything shattered.

I was awakened out of a deep sleep by two distinct sounds I will never forget. I would soon find out that the love of my life, my sweetheart, my husband, best friend, lover, and father of my children was taken in the blink of an eye. Without any warning, he left us.

I heard it. It was a snatching, a taking. A rapture.

A purposeful and supernatural act of God.

Epic. So fitting a transition to the eternal realm for such an amazing visionary and creative dreamer. He didn't step over... he flew! He shot up out of this earthly body and flew. I know it.

Death. It's a certainty for every human being.

We all have that appointment waiting for us, we just don't know when it will take place.

We've all thought of the possibility of the one we love leaving this earth someday. Although we don't ever really want to think about it, it crosses your mind. It's a fleeting thought that is pushed aside quickly saying, "Not now, there's so much yet to be lived out." I never imagined it would be like this. I sincerely believed with all my heart it would be much later in life. Much later.

For David William Smith, "my Dave" it was this day, this hour in the middle of the night after a beautiful Thanksgiving Day at only 50 years old.

We had so many plans and dreams that yet needed to be fulfilled.

Now he was gone in the blink of an eye.

My treasure. My sweetness. My heart. My best friend.

Dreams for continued happiness and love caved in on me... in an instant.

I want to share the details because I feel it is important. God doesn't do anything by accident and nothing, not even the most tragic pain, will be allowed to be for naught.

Dave's departure from this earth was purposeful. That word alone describes what I have stood on since the moment the nurse came in and told me he was gone...purposeful.

I sensed it immediately even in the dark fog that surrounded my thoughts and understanding. The shadow of death could not block out the Son's intention. Purposeful means "full of purpose". God was in this. Even this. There will be purpose.

My husband always knew God was in the details. He said it all the time. Now I knew I had to find God in the details of this potentially devastating part of our story.

From the first moments of this tragic event,
I chose to believe there was purpose even in this.
I have to believe even now that my husband's death
and my pain will not be in vain.
God doesn't waste pain.
He uses everything.
Even ashes.

I'm Mad at Spring

Have you ever been angry at Spring? I am.
So, here's a look into the grieving process
that has taken me by surprise.
I'm angry at spring.

Yes, I'm angry at the warm breeze, the sunshine,
the flowers in bloom, the green in the trees, the birds chirping,
and every single bug that is buzzing around. Angry.
I was content with grey skies, cold wind, and dead fauna.
At least then, everything around me seemed to be
feeling my heart.

Today as I walked into a home improvement
store's garden section,
spring slapped me in the face.
It felt like the sky and earth and everything
in between was smiling and it made me mad.
Do "they" not know my Dave is gone?!
When it was still cold and grey it felt like nature
was still with me.

It felt like at least the earth had not forgotten.
It was somehow feeling my pain.
But with spring comes the obvious fact that
everything is moving on, moving forward.
People, insects, plants, and flowers... all moving on with life,
while I am still sitting here grieving the one I love.

It doesn't feel right or fair.
It hurts and I'm mad.
There's a huge piece of reality for you.
I'm mad at spring.
Yes, I know it's a natural, healthy part of life... but today,
I don't like it at all.
Yes, I love God with all my heart.
He knows I'm mad at spring, and He's not mad at me for it.
He's abounding in love and compassion towards me today.

—

Just as a father has compassion on his children, so the LORD has compassion on those who fear Him. For He Himself knows our frame; He is mindful that we are but dust.

—Psalm 103:13-14 NASB

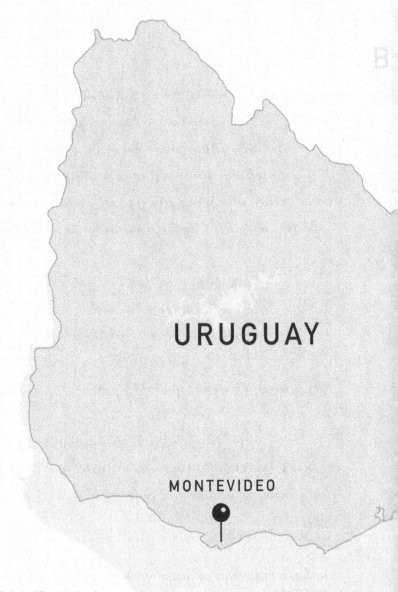

My Beginning

Montevideo, Uruguay, is the second smallest country in South America. It shares its borders with Argentina and Brazil. Its culture has heavy European influence, its food is the best, its language is Spanish, and its people are passionate about pretty much everything, especially soccer. That's where I was born. My beginning. But first, let me go a little further back and introduce you to my parents.

Aurora Casal and Alfredo Rodriguez were only 16 and 17 when they married on December 18, 1954. Both came from poor homes and families riddled with dysfunction. They had their first child just five months after their courthouse ceremony. My brother Alfredo was born in May of 1955. Only 11 months would pass before the April 1956 arrival of my sister, Graciela. I wouldn't make my appearance until 10 years later.

In those ten years, my young naïve mother would be forced to abort seven other babies. My father's mother, Josefa, aided and abetted my father's many affairs, even making a room in her home for him to bring women to. It was a very immoral and toxic atmosphere that was considered normal to my father's side of the family. In those days, macho men just did what they did and there was no room to question it.

Regarding the pregnancies, my paternal grandmother convinced my mother and father over and over that it would be best to just get rid of each "inconvenience" since they struggled enough to feed the two they already had. All this while welcoming his many trysts into her own house. Josefa resented the fact that her young son had decided to be tied down at such an early age. After all, he had so much living to do and women to conquer. In regards to aborting the babies, my grandmother would tell my mother, "It's just a blob of flesh anyway."

My mother wasn't sure if that was true. As a matter of fact, she felt in her heart that they were tiny human beings. She did not know any better and had no one in her life to give her caring advice. From the first to the last abortion, she was never asked if this was what she wanted. She was never included in the decision she was making for her own body. She was only told the date and time it would happen, then taken to a clinic. Her first abortion was without anesthesia of any kind. To this day she recalls the horrible and painful experience with tears of regret. Sometimes the procedures were done at home by strangers called upon by my father's family. Today, my mother will tell you that she was completely clueless about life. She had no idea that she could possibly have a voice or opinion. Living in poverty, ignorance, and fear, she convinced herself that it would be best for those little souls that were formed in her womb not to be born into the hell she was living in. With the encouragement of my father, his mother, and aunts, she was made to go through with what she really didn't want to do in her heart. Seven times.

She remembers crying, placing her hands on her belly, and asking the baby inside her to forgive her for what she was about to do or had just done.

After her seventh abortion, she remembers walking home alone and talking to a God she didn't know intimately yet, but believed was out there somewhere. "God, I will never do this again. I don't care if I get pregnant 10 more times. I will never kill another one of my children."

Not long after that conversation with God in 1965, my mother discovered she was pregnant again by the abusive husband she both loved and feared. She decided in her heart that this time would be different. She would keep her promise to God. Courageously standing against what anyone would tell her, she would give this baby life. I was that baby. She never got pregnant again.

On March 25, 1966, I took my first breath on this earth and began the journey God set out for me, with the family He chose for me.

When my mother discovered that she was pregnant once again and made the decision to spare my life, she vowed to God that she would dedicate my life to Him as a symbol of her contrition for the babies she'd been forced to give up. Thus, Maria was chosen as my middle name in honor of Jesus' mother, Mary.

My mother told me that such was her desire to honor God with my life that if I had been a boy, she would have named me Jesus. In honor of the American dream she so longed for, my mother named me Jacqueline. I was named after the beautiful and famous American first lady who then was a symbol of the height of fashion and grace and was admired by the world.

My earliest memories as a toddler are sad and dark. My father's drunken rages always resulted in screaming insults and punches thrown. These terrible, ongoing events often culminated in some kind of bloody altercation, my mother crying, and me hiding in fear under the bed. I wished with all my heart that dad would not drink alcohol. I begged him not to. He had no control when he was drunk. His jealous rage, outrageous allegations, and imaginations caused so much pain for his wife and children. In the years that followed, we all had to deal with the emotional scars and traumas we endured as children. We suffered at the hands of a man controlled by alcohol and the excuse of machismo. I believe my mother's pure and sincere faith in the face of turmoil, abuse, and poverty was what kept her sane.

She always believed and hoped that somehow God would make things better.

In the '60s, the United States of America was the destination my parents dreamt about. It was the booming land of opportunity and progress where they longed to go to live a better life. In 1969, my father traveled to the US for the first time with a tourist visa. He then went back and forth for several more years before our whole family was able to receive legal residency. We immigrated to the little town of Ossining, New York in 1972. Moving to the United States was an exciting whirlwind. I was thrust into a world that had different weather, ate different food, and spoke a different language. I was fascinated by the snowy winters and loved American food and culture, but my biggest hurdle was learning the language. I was determined to learn it quickly and correctly. My goal at just six years old was to speak English without an accent. Even then, I remember thinking, "If this is going to be my country, I will honor it by speaking, reading, and writing in perfect English." My mother recollects that only three months after arriving in the United States she heard me talking to a friend over the telephone in fluent English. She was so proud of me.

My parents sent me to a Catholic school for our first few years in the United States, where I learned many different prayers. My favorite, and one I said before going to sleep at night, was the Lord's Prayer. I appreciated that it encompassed everything I wanted to say to God, not even knowing the context in which Jesus had actually said, "This is the way you should pray" about this specific prayer. No one ever taught me that you could just talk to God like a friend... but late at night, when all the lights were turned off for the day, I felt the invitation in my heart that I could. So I did. I talked to God. I knew He was out there somewhere and that He was listening.

In those early years in America, one of my favorite things to do was to visit the library and find books that helped me learn new words in English. I loved Richard Scarry's "best" book series. My favorite one was Richard Scarry's Best Word Book Ever. I studied that particular one in depth, and it helped me learn most of my very first English words. There was something so magical to me about the colorful animal characters in their little human clothes doing all kinds of busy things in their busy little towns. I spent hours poring over the illustrations in search of the tiny, smiling worm hidden throughout the pages. In addition to those wonderful books, television shows like Sesame Street, The Electric Company, and Zoom helped me to further grasp this new American language and culture.

In 1977, my family moved to South Florida to be closer to my sister, her husband, Jorge, and their new baby girl. I loved growing up in Fort Lauderdale. My mother embraced the warmer weather of the South, especially in comparison to the gray and snowy winter months in New York. Although my family had moved to a much better location, our dysfunction continued. My father still got drunk, hit my mother, and had affairs. My mom remained submissive in the most negative sense of the word. Our home was still hell on earth, only now it was just better dressed.

As I grew, making friends gave me a reason to venture out of the house more often. I especially loved attending teen discos at the local recreation center. Dancing with my friends became a happy escape from my sad home. It was there that the soundtrack of my life transformed from angry shouting and violent outbursts to the joyful sounds of the Bee Gees, Kool and the Gang, and other popular music of the time.

We were never particularly religious in our home, but there was always a blanketed belief in God's existence. Although we'd say we were Catholic if someone asked, we only attended mass or church if there was a wedding. Despite this, you could definitely say we were all "seekers." My sister Grace and her husband tried out several different religions before truly finding a personal relationship with Jesus. Once they found Jesus and accepted him into their lives, they were ALL in. Grace invited my mother and me to attend a special service on Valentine's night at a small Spanish storefront church. That church is where I learned for the first time that Jesus loved me and wanted to have a relationship with me. After the preacher got done with his sermon, he invited those that wanted to ask Jesus into their hearts to come forward.

Although I had been greatly moved by the new revelation that the Son of God loved & wanted to know ME, this wasn't a phrase I was familiar with. I was unsure of what the preacher was inviting us to do. After a minute or two of contemplating the meaning of "asking Jesus into my heart" the invitation became clear to me when a kind, elderly woman sat beside me and asked if I'd like to receive Jesus as my personal Savior and Friend. Finally, fully understanding the life-changing decision before me, I said, "Yes." I still remember thinking in that moment, "Who wouldn't want to?" She gently took my hand and guided me up to the altar to pray. On February 14, 1980, Jesus became my best friend and forever Valentine. I've never looked back.

My mother and I began attending the little storefront church with my sister and her family. Eventually, my brother and sister-in-law attended as well. My father began to hear and see the Gospel lived out before him through the lives of his wife and children. My mother found worth in Jesus and finally stood up to my father demanding he never lift his hand at her again. Miraculously, he didn't ever hit her again. Although the physical abuse in my home slowly diminished, when he drank too much, dad continued to be boisterous and violent with his words, especially directed at my mother.

We sometimes saw glimpses of his potential to be a good man. He began to realize that his early life choices had some huge consequences in his relationship with his now adult children. Although we always gathered for family events and holidays, things were strained between dad and me and my siblings. As the grandchildren came along, my father softened and was everything as a grandfather to them that he was not as a father to us. It was nice to see him interact in a fun and loving way with his grandchildren. Even with all the childhood pain I endured, I loved my dad and respected his role, but I struggled with hate for him as well. I think most children raised in an abusive home feel the same way. There was a huge struggle between love and hate that continuously gnawed at me. Over the years, I begged God to help me forgive my dad.

My father was not a great father. He was not the kind of dad that was caring, tender, protective, or prone to reading bedtime stories. He was a man with his own issues—alcohol, violent behavior, and womanizing being some of them. How does a human become this kind of a man, husband and father?

It all starts in childhood.

My father was not parented in a nurturing atmosphere. He was brought up in a very poor and dysfunctional home where it was normal to tell little boys what their private parts were made for. He was born and raised in a household that exalted promiscuity and vices. The macho mentality reigned and you were considered a real man if you had a lot of conquests.

Along with being taught how to live in all the wrong ways by the negative influences around him, he grew up angry and bitter towards the things he saw and experienced as a little boy. I never understood why he had turned out this way, and I never truly forgave him until we had a conversation I'll never forget.

He'd been hospitalized many times because of complications

with emphysema due to smoking. This habit took his last breath only a year later. He was in a hospital bed when I came to see him one afternoon. With misty eyes and a far off look, he confessed a few secrets and hidden experiences from his childhood that brought quick understanding to my mind. One of the many things he told me was that one day when he was just seven years old, he saw something terrible take place in his home that scarred him for the rest of his life. Traumatized, confused and full of rage he ran and ran until he couldn't run anymore. Completely exhausted, with tears running down his cheeks, he finally stopped running and with clenched fists to the sky, he vowed to "hurt every woman" that came into his life.

As he painted this sad memory with his words, my heart broke for a physically and emotionally abused little boy from long ago. For the first time, I saw my dad as a weak and sad man full of regrets. As we talked, he added with a deep sigh, "Oh! I wish I could go back and change things. I would do so many things differently." That was one of the most profound "aha!" moments of my life. A conversation I would never forget.

All the awful life experiences my mother, siblings, and I suffered throughout our lives suddenly made sense. It became clear to me in that moment that my father's childhood secret affected all of us. All my warped memories of a drunk and violent father came into clear focus. The man who was unfaithful to my mother and inadvertently taught me to never trust anyone was once a hurt little boy. This little boy grew up to be a deeply wounded man who would, in turn, hurt others. He wasn't shown or taught what true love looked like, so he didn't know how to love. The saying, "hurt people hurt people" is so true. That confession and deep expression of a wounded soul was what helped me forgive him wholly.

Dad had accepted Christ as Savior years prior, but he never truly surrendered his life until many years later on his deathbed in 2007.

The decades of alcohol abuse and cigarette smoking finally caught up to him. This strong man who always wanted to be in charge had now succumbed to emphysema and cirrhosis of the liver. Now the illnesses were in charge and his body began shutting down. They had to intubate him so he could breathe. One of the saddest and hardest moments of my life was having to translate the doctor's words to Spanish, "There is nothing else we can do for you". My father looked at me with a heartbroken expression and asked, "Nothing?" I shook my head and cried. My heart truly hurt for this weak and broken man before me.

My most fervent prayer in those last days was for dad to have the courage to ask mom for forgiveness. He had never uttered the words, "I'm sorry" to her in his whole life. I was so happy to find out that one afternoon as I stepped out of his hospital room to get some coffee, Dad motioned for Mom to come close. When she did, he struggled to whisper, "I always loved you. Forgive me." That's all she needed to hear.

The next morning I walked into his hospital room to find him sitting up in his bed, just staring. Dad said, "Jesus and I had a long conversation last night. I told him that if it was my time to go, it was ok with me. I'm ready."

Just a few days later with my mother at his side, dad took his last breath on this earth on February 23, 2007. Redemption doesn't always look like we imagine, but when it finally arrives—even in the last moments of life—it is beautiful.

I can't wait for the day I step into forever and see my father waiting for me! Healed and whole. We have a lot of catching up to do.

Let the redeemed of the Lord tell their story, those He redeemed from the hand of the foe, those He gathered from the lands, from east and west, from north and south.

—Psalm 107:2-3 NIV

Our Love Story, Our Beginning

I'm hungrier for heaven than I've ever been.

That's because half of me is already there.

When you have experienced true love the way I have, there's nothing that can take its place when it is gone. Covenant love is something truly unique; it is a gift from God. Covenant love is sincere, intentional, selfless, and deep. Covenant love lasts beyond death. Covenant love is eternal. It's more than a sweet story or a beautiful song. It is real, deep, and alive. I experienced that kind of love.

Knowing my love language to be words, my husband applied a wall decal over our bed that reads, "Every love story is beautiful, but ours is my favorite."

Our love story began in the summer of 1985. I was smitten by David William Smith, an 18-year-old Ft. Lauderdale Art Institute student from Jacksonville, Florida, and the new guy in the youth group. Talented, sweet, and handsome, he stole my heart the first day I met him in the young adult Sunday school class. At that time in my life, I was feeling quite blessed to be the only female in the class. Conveniently for me, I was the one taking roll that morning. I made sure to learn this cute guy's name, which was important in case he came back. I made a mental note in addition to writing it down—all for hospitality's sake, of course. I mean, David Smith was not a hard name to remember; even more importantly, I realized quickly it was a name I didn't want to forget.

The next time I saw him was on a Wednesday evening at church. He had come back at the end of summer with his mother. She drove down to help move her son into the apartment he'd be living in while in college. I said hello and greeted him by name. He was impressed that I remembered him. Sporting a mullet and cool confidence, David stood out from the other guys. The fact that he was wearing a white tuxedo shirt with tails, jeans, and wrestler boots made him king of '80s fashion. He often wore a tee shirt and white blazer a la Tubbs and Crocket. Miami Vice had nothing on him.

As we got to know him, my friends and I learned rather quickly that the new skinny kid's talents weren't limited to the comic book heroes he could easily sketch or the way he could magically use a spray paint can like a paintbrush. David could turn a simple bed sheet into a canvas for a skit backdrop in no time. His wheelhouse pretty much was anything artistically inspired.

David was a great actor, too. He could portray a troubled gang member, a high school jock, a nerd, or an evil devil. He took any acting challenge and became the character. David Smith was always "all in." He never did anything halfway. For the rest of his life, he continued to say, "Do it right or don't do it at all," which became one of his many mottos that he lived out until his last breath.

We came to find out that David could also do everyone's makeup for any drama or skit the group was putting on. He could apply stage makeup like a pro! He could turn a young person into an old person in a matter of minutes with just some baby powder and eyeliner. Nasty fake cuts, scrapes, and bruises? No problem! Just hand him some blue eyeshadow and red lipstick. Done!

This is the career path he actually wanted to specialize in after graduating high school, but some well-meaning, yet religious church people told him he couldn't do it. They said that Christians didn't move to Hollywood to become movie makeup artists. That would be worldly and wrong. Apparently, they didn't see it as a holy endeavor to use your "God-given" talent in a way that would somehow be connected to the secular stage.

David later told me that he couldn't understand this way of thinking. He actually thought instead, "What better way to use my talents? I could potentially have an actor in my chair for hours at a time and could speak to them, encourage them, and influence them just by being present in their lives while doing makeup." He abandoned his dream of doing movie makeup early on since it was frowned upon by church people. You don't learn until much later in life that people's opinions shouldn't matter when you know what God is asking you to do. Everyone has a unique calling and it's ok if the crowds don't "get it." It's not their calling, it's yours.

Our youth group also discovered that David Smith could sing. We came to find out that this young stranger could hit high notes the likes of Michael Sweet of Stryper fame. David often sang in the youth group. Those were the days of cassette accompaniment tracks. "Medals" by Russ Taff was a favorite. I can see him now, wearing his white parachute pants and red suspenders. He had this thing where he would stand with his legs just a little apart and shake his right leg to the beat of the song. Oh, he was so cool! For a short-lived time, he was also a part of a Christian rock band made up of a bunch of mullet-sporting buds from the youth group. The '80s were a lot of fun and everyone who met him loved David Smith.

David and I quickly became friends and eventually, best friends. Our friendship suffered some ups and downs during the following two years, while I waited (impatiently) for him to graduate, because he promised God he wouldn't date while he was in college. David told me he made this promise to God because he felt he needed to "focus only on school." In spite of my prodding, he actually kept his word. This was a sign of things to come; David Smith, a faithful promise keeper to the end. He said he wouldn't date anyone for those two years and he didn't.

This made me mad. At the time, I could only see what I

selfishly wanted. Why did he go and promise God something like this? Why couldn't he date me and go to college at the same time? Why couldn't he just tell God he made a mistake by making such a silly promise and take it back?

Our love story began as a flirtatious friendship in the youth group that grew cold for a season because of my impatience. It wasn't until much later that I understood that my behavior was because of "daddy issues." The lack of affirmation and attention from a loving father in my own life turned me into a young lady needy for attention and love. I subconsciously thought that having the affection or attention of a boy would give me my worth. I was looking for the value I didn't get from daddy. In turn, if a boy I had a crush on didn't like me back, I was devastated and blamed myself for not looking pretty enough or whatever enough. I had no idea at the time that this was an internal issue I needed to deal with. It was just the way it was.

Since David didn't want to date me or anyone else for that matter, I decided I would go out with someone else. Yeah, stupid decision, but it made complete sense in my 19-year-old mind. I needed affirmation and resented what I perceived to be a personal rejection.

Enter Mitchell, a tall, handsome, law school student. Mitchell had a flirtatious, sheepish smile that could win you over in an instant. He was great with poetic words that could melt a young lady's heart. He was very sweet, and we enjoyed hanging out together. Regardless of all his good qualities, we were not meant to be.

One afternoon Mitchell and I drove up to church for something and David was walking across the parking lot. I must have stared a little too long because Mitchell looked at me and declared, "You're in love with David Smith." I denied it. But as time would tell, he was right.

It was Labor Day 1987, at the end of a church picnic, when I finally realized that Mitchell wasn't the one for me. After a fun day full of friends, barbecues, and games, I felt empty. Mitchell had to drive back to college that afternoon. I vividly remember the moment we said our nonchalant goodbyes. It kind of startled me as he drove off that I wasn't sad about him leaving. All I could think about was how mad I was that David didn't seem to care I was dating Mitchell. It was in this moment that I realized, "This is a waste of time. What am I doing?" I had only tried to make this work because of my own insecurities and the need to be loved. It wasn't fair to Mitchell, and it wasn't fair to me.

As I drove down I-95 on the way home, I cried and cried because I knew I had to break up with Mitchell. But I was crying for the wrong reasons. I knew God was telling me this was a relationship based on a false need to be accepted and cared for. I cried because I was scared to break up with him. What if no one else ever loved me? I looked up to the sky through my tears and said out loud, "God, I'm afraid of being alone!" He heard me.

God, I'm afraid of being alone!

Just an hour or so later I found myself at a friend's house for our weekly get together. A group of young adults—some married, some single—had started meeting on Monday evenings at this friend's apartment for snacks, Bible study, and prayer. After hanging out and chatting for a while, we all ended up sitting on the living room floor in a circle. Some suggested specific things we could pray about. I was quiet. All I could think about was my honest conversation with God in the car. I was truly afraid of being alone. We began praying out loud one at a time for whatever needs or things that settled in our hearts. David Smith wasn't there that night, but another friend named David began to pray. He blurted out nervously, "I feel like God put some things on my heart to say to each of you. I hope I'm hearing right, but here goes." He went around and spoke a short word of encouragement to each person. When he came to me, with tears in his eyes he said, "Jackie, the Lord just says, 'Don't be afraid of being alone.'"

Wait, what?! My friend had no idea what I had said to God in the car an hour earlier. In that moment, I knew God was serious about me doing what I knew I had to do, break up with Mitchell. On the way home that night I purposed in my heart that I would obey God and not be afraid to be alone. I knew that I wasn't alone anyway if I had God with me. A second serious conversation in the car with God began. "If I never find love or get married, it doesn't matter. I'm ok with just you and me, God. You're all I need." I really meant it. I didn't have a clue that my sincere prayer would be the catalyst to finding my forever love in the next 24 hours.

I went home that night and called Mitchell on the telephone. It went something like this. "Mitchell, I'm so sorry, but I really feel like we're supposed to break up."

His response? "Okay." Click. He hung up on me! Well, that settled that. Apparently, he didn't care for me like I thought he did. A wave of peace washed over me. I looked up and smiled.

The next evening there was a gathering at church. As I was leaving, my friend Vickie called out to me. "Hey Jackie, do you have a minute? I have a question. Are you still dating Mitchell?" "No, actually, I broke up with him last night. God told me to," I said with a big smile. I was so relieved and thankful to have obeyed God the night before.

Vickie continued, "Oh, that's good because I didn't know how I was going to tell you this, but he's been talking to someone else."

What should have devastated me in that moment only made me smile at the thought that God already knew what I now knew. My obedience, albeit reluctant, had saved me from embarrassment and heartbreak. I thanked Vickie for being honest and straightforward with me. "This is a good friend," I thought as I almost floated away towards my car knowing all was well. Looking up at the sky I thought to myself, "It's just you and me, God and I'm okay with that."

As I walked back across the parking lot, who came strolling out of the church? None other than the one and only David Smith. My heart skipped a beat at the sight of him. *God, no. We just decided it was just You and me now*, I thought to myself.

David came straight towards me and called out, "Hey, how are you?" I had just seen him the day before at the picnic, but it felt like an eternity. I was so happy to see him again! As he neared, I knew we'd hug hello, and we did. It was one of those extra special hugs that say a million words in a second or two, with an added squeeze at the end before letting go. We both looked at each other silently and awkwardly for a second because somehow in that moment we realized our relationship was about to take a significant turn.

The conversation quickly went from "I just graduated from the Art Institute last week",

"Oh, cool. Congratulations" to "How are you and Mitchell doing?" "Oh, we just broke up"... silence...

"Hey, we haven't talked in a long time, we need to catch up."

"Yeah, you should call me later."

"I'll call you when I get home." He did.

That phone call literally lasted all night. We talked about everything, including the fact that we had always loved each other and we were meant to be, what our first dog's name would be and how David would design our dream home some day. What started out as friendship, instantaneously grew stronger that night and "Can't Fight This Feeling" by REO Speedwagon became 'our song'.

As the sun came up, we realized we had a lifetime of dreams to fulfill and didn't want to spend another day apart.

It really would have been ok with it just being God and me, but I am forever grateful that His plan was for it to be God, David, and me all along.

Now, as it turns out, it's back to just God and me and I have to be ok with that. Once again I say, "I will not be afraid of being alone."

Literally, at the very moment I am writing this, an unexpected ding on the computer indicates there's a message from an amazing young man who is a friend of the family. It reads, "Hey Aunt Jackie! Just felt led to tell you I love you and you have a big calling on your life! God is going to use you in ways you won't believe because He says He will never leave you!!"

And there you have it…. God speaks to me once again, the same message He spoke all those years ago. His promise still stands. He will never leave me, and I won't be afraid of being alone.

Be strong! Be fearless! Don't be afraid and don't be scared by your enemies, because the Lord your God is the one who marches with you. He won't let you down, and he won't abandon you.

—Deuteronomy 31:5-7 CSB

Intentional Life,
Intentional Marriage

———————— ❧ ————————

We dated for six months. We were engaged for six months after.

One year and two weeks after that all-night phone conversation, we were married on a beautiful, sunny, Saturday afternoon in 1988. September 24th would become my favorite date until forever.

Our love story had a sweet beginning, a beautiful middle, but will never have an end. It was as perfect as two imperfect people could ever hope for. An epic life of promises fulfilled, covenant kept, and the deep love some have only dreamt of.

We were a good team...No, I take that back. We were a great team! It was always "Dave and Jackie." Whether in marriage, ministry, friendships, or family—it was always "Dave and Jackie." We were a package deal. Always.

We even said this to the first pastor that ever hired "us" although technically they were just hiring him on staff at the time. I told that pastor that he was getting a great "two-for-one" deal because we knew that whatever we set out to do, we would do together. Interestingly, pointing at Dave, that pastor said, "Yes, but just to be clear, we're only hiring him." Yeah, they were only "paying" him, but we did it together regardless of a paycheck. They really did get a good deal!

We loved being together. We would often say how we didn't understand couples that needed "time away from one another". We hated being apart. The longest we were ever apart in marriage was ten days, when I traveled to Europe with my mother and sister. As much fun as that trip was, I couldn't wait to be back in his arms. This is why now this eternal, unknown length of "temporal" separation is so difficult for me.

Dave and I entered marriage knowing we were both completely "in." We knew it would take work and effort. A lot of people go into marriage knowing that it will take work, but don't think to be intentional about it. We were thoughtfully intentional in planning the work and effort a healthy marriage would take.

Our first intentional step was to understand that having a "like faith" in Jesus and shared values were the foundation of everything we'd build moving forward.

We declared from the beginning that God would always be at the center of our home. That's where our love would be planted. Jesus would be the best soil to be rooted in. We understood and believed with all our hearts that our love and commitment to Him first would spill into our marriage and help us walk out our promises.

We also understood that to make our marriage successful, we'd have to do things differently than what we saw and lived through as children.

We'd have to feed and water our marriage with respect, faithfulness, and understanding for it to blossom into what we did not see in our homes growing up.

Both our fathers were alcoholics and "womanizers" as Dave would call them.

My father, a violent drunk; his, a quiet drunk, both allowing the abuse of alcohol to ruin their marriages. His mother took out her anger on the kitchen cabinets, slamming them and yelling when angry; mine suffered quietly and endured internally, her suffering taking shape in the form of physical bruises as well. Dave's parents' marriage ended in divorce when he was 5 years old, while my parents stayed unhappily married for 52 years. Their stories are an entirely different book for another time.

Having both grown up with these bad examples for relationship and marriage, we talked through what we would change in our own marriage. We determined to be intentional in the way we planned, prepared, and lived out our married life. We would be intentional in talking things out together moving forward no matter what the future brought our way.

From the beginning, we wanted to be intentional in our approach to marriage, meaning that we would do things on purpose and deliberately to feed what we wanted to grow. If our marriage was to not only survive like many do, but thrive, take root, and produce beautiful fruit, we had to be intentional in all the aspects of this journey.

I have always said that I didn't have the home I would have wanted or dreamt of growing up, but MY home as a wife and mother could be the home of my dreams. Dave agreed and together we set out to make that happen.

Intentionally, we set out to plant and grow a marriage that we could be proud of at the end of our days. A marriage our children would want to model theirs after.

We talked a lot about what was bad growing up. We talked about some of the good. We discussed what we could learn from all of it.

We prayed together and asked God to help us forgive and break any generational curses that came along with our family lineages.

We committed to each other that our children would never experience violence, unfaithfulness, or disrespect as we had experienced.

We promised to never speak harshly to each other or call each other names, not even in jest. We promised never to throw around the word divorce, neither as a joke or a threat. We promised that when disagreements came, as we knew they would, we would communicate like adults, walking away to "separate corners" if angry, until we could discuss things calmly and come to an agreement.

Dave was such a great gauge and balance to my black-and-white decision making process. I hardly ever spent or purchased anything without counting the cost, researching all options, and thinking it through. Praying the whole time for direction that I was doing the right thing. *God, do I really need this purse? It's cute, but is it practical? I have other purses in my closet. What if I need that $30 for something more important tomorrow?* I'd walk around the store with it and end up putting it back. Dave's response most of the time was, "Do you like it? Will you make use of it? Then get it, Bear (his nickname for me). God always provides. Money comes and money goes. God will give us what we need when we need it." He not only had complete faith and confidence that the $30 purse would not break or bankrupt us, but also that if it put a smile on my face, it was totally worth it.

When purchasing a gift for someone, I considered: *Do they need it? Will they use it? Is it practical?* He would instead make gift purchases based on his thoughts of, *will they love it? Will it make them happy? Will it make them smile? Is it something they'd never buy for themselves?*

So thoughtful, caring, and detailed were his gifts that I always joked that he always "one-upped me" in that department.

When tipping at a restaurant, my thinking was, *Were they attentive? Did the server have a bad attitude?* His philosophy was, "Honey, tip the girl, You don't know what she's going through. She's probably having a bad day. God sees. God knows. God will give it back to us."

This type of thinking showed my sense of justice and his sense of mercy. We never thought the other person was wrong for thinking or feeling the way they did. We just embraced their point of view and when combined with our own, it would most often produce a good and balanced decision. This is why I believe we were a great team. We appreciated and embraced our differences and celebrated our unique backgrounds and understanding of things. We leaned into each other's strengths and helped the other in their weakness. Looking back I can smile with satisfaction at our marriage. I am beyond thankful.

As the wife in the relationship, I knew that there may be times when our opinions differed on how something should be handled, but I also knew that at the end of the day, as the head of the home, he'd be responsible to God for the final decision. Because of this, I defered to him. Thankfully, this hardly ever happened because we did agree on just about everything. But even if we didn't, we talked it out calmly until we came to an agreement.

One of the many great things Dave did was listen. He wouldn't just say, "I'm the man, and it's my way." He'd intently listen to my thoughts and opinions about things and then we'd always come to an understanding. We learned that marriage is a balancing act of equal parts unselfishness. It can never be just one way or mostly one way. It has to be a sweet, intentional surrender to the fulfillment and joy of the other. If both partners do this, everyone's happy. We were happy... very happy for 29 years and exactly 2 months of marriage.

Dave often said, "In marriage, both partners have to put work into it. It's not 50/50, it's 100/100." And I can truly attest that from day one, we tried our best to live that way every day. In this crazy life, with all the challenges it brings, some days were easier than others. However, one thing is for certain, we loved each other so deeply that we never wanted to hurt one another. Having that as a basis for everyday living helped us keep the vows we made long ago. Consideration. Respect. Honor. Those are words to live by in marriage or any relationship.

I have always been more vocal and outwardly passionate about things, but his patient and quiet demeanor taught me so much over the years. We allowed life experiences and how we each responded to them to balance our own responses. Now that he's gone, I find myself saying, "What would Dave say?" in any given situation. Dave had so much quiet wisdom and discernment. In decision making, we were always a team. Me the "practical, get all the information and think through everything" person and he the "generous, forgiving, patient, and understanding give it all away person". Whether it was gift-giving, tipping a waitress, large purchases, giving in benevolence, or buying anything, big or small, we were always intentionally aware and cared about the other one's feelings, thoughts, and opinions on the matter.

Being intentional each and every day in the way you love and care for someone is not an easy task, but Dave Smith did it so well. Maybe it was his artistic eye for detail, but he was detailed even in the way he played out his role as husband.

He taught me what it truly means to be unselfish and generous, patient, and kind.

His intentional love for me in our everyday normal is what I miss the most.

The following passage in the Bible expresses how Dave learned to love me. I like it best translated in The Message Bible. It is Ephesians 5:25-28,

"Husbands, go all out in your love for your wives, exactly as Christ did for the church—a love marked by giving, not getting. Christ's love makes the church whole. His words evoke her beauty. Everything he does and says is designed to bring the best out of her, dressing her in dazzling white silk, radiant with holiness. And that is how husbands ought to love their wives. They're really doing themselves a favor—since they're already "one" in marriage." (The Message)

Christ's love for His "bride," which is comprised of all those that love Him and have committed themselves to Him, is captured in these few verses. Jesus loves us unconditionally, unselfishly, and completely. This is how Paul admonishes husbands to love their wives. This is how my husband loved me. He not only loved me well but also lived love in front of others. He loved his children, family, and friends well.

No matter how tired, weary, or exhausted he may have been, his love was in action in an instant if we needed him. He never complained. True love puts itself aside when someone needs a hand, encouragement, or companionship. He never, ever told me he was too tired to do something for me. He never denied me his attention or care.

Dave loved a lot of things. He loved communicating God's love to children. He loved unfolding the truths of God's Word in themes, stories, and object lessons. He loved a creative challenge.

He loved excellence, adventure, and fun. He loved an epic action-adventure story. He loved imagination and artistry. His life was full of love.

The everyday kind of love that doesn't need to show off.

The love that gives and asks nothing in return.

The kind of love that just is.

Even when it came to gift-giving, he was the best. Again, he was so meticulous. Whether wrapping a gift or decorating for our birthdays, he was all about the thoughtful details. When there was a birthday in the house, he'd stay up as late as necessary to hang a curtain of streamers on your bedroom door so that'd be the first thing that greeted you on your birthday morning. He would take care to remember and make a mental note of things I liked and without fail, even when I had forgotten, I'd find that very thing wrapped under the Christmas tree. He sincerely found joy in making people smile.

Dave would do anything for his kids at the drop of a hat. He often joked with us saying, "I give and I give and I give, and what do I get? Nothing." We would all dramatically say, "Nothing" in unison with him. We'd all laugh, but it was actually true. I mean the giving and giving part, not the "nothing" part. We did give back to him a lot of love, hugs, kisses, and thank yous. We loved him more than he could have ever imagined. We appreciated him more than he could have ever comprehended. Even more so now that he's gone we realize the huge treasure he was each and every day.

I do wish I would have told him just one more time how amazing he was to me.

A friend of ours recently said to me, "When I read this passage in the Message Bible, I thought of Dave. This really describes him."

The passage was 1 Corinthians 13.

"Love never gives up.
Love cares more for others than for self.
Love doesn't want what it doesn't have.
Love doesn't strut,
Doesn't have a swelled head,
Doesn't force itself on others,
Isn't always "me first,"
Doesn't fly off the handle,
Doesn't keep score of the sins of others,
Doesn't revel when others grovel,
Takes pleasure in the flowering of truth,
Puts up with anything,
Trusts God always,
Always looks for the best,
Never looks back,
But keeps going to the end." (The Message)

My Dave sure did love like Jesus!
Intentionally!.

What a great example he set for me, his kids,
and everyone who had the opportunity
to know him.

Yes, darling, you gave and gave and gave...
and what did you get?

Heaven!

The Calling

———— ⊙⊷⊙ ————

The Smith family began attending Southside Assembly of God in 1973. A few years later, Dave's older brother Duane became a children's pastor. Little David was recruited to help his big brother in children's church. At just 9 years old, Dave began performing various puppet characters during Sunday morning services. In the years that followed, Duane continued to fan the flames of creativity in his younger brother by giving him many opportunities to perform, design puppets, and create sets for his ministry events. I remember many phone calls from Duane that began with, "Hey baby brother, I have an idea!" Duane was a pioneer in children's ministry and made a great impact on his younger brother's life.

Although those early ministry experiences held very special memories for Dave, he never planned to be a minister.

Since the mid-'80s, Dave and I were very involved in anything and everything having to do with church. Our life revolved around activities and friendships in the church. There we found a strong group of friends that always hung out together. True community.

If we weren't in church, we were hanging out at someone's house, meeting up to eat somewhere, or going to the movies. These were the days before texting. Just the good old-fashioned, curly cord, hanging on the kitchen wall telephone days. We'd call one or two people and say. "We're going to so-and-so's house tonight" and have them pass it on.

They would call a couple of other people and by the end of the day, there would be 20-30 young people having fun, engaged in some sort of '80s-style shenanigans. Whether toilet papering someone's house, miniature golf, Polaroid scavenger hunts, or arcade game hangs, our group of friends always had a good time.

As young adults, before and up to a couple of years after getting married, Dave and I both volunteered in the youth ministry as leaders. We were in choirs, musicals, cantatas, dramas, skits, and talent shows. If there was anything creative going on, you'd find us there. Dave built sets, backdrops, and props. He'd spend countless hours fabricating and painting. Sometimes he'd work on sets all night long. When he was creating, he'd lose track of time and just keep going to get it "just right." He'd do this for the rest of his life.

The "calling" came during a Sunday evening service. An evangelist by the name of Danny DuVall was the guest speaker at our home church, Christian Life Center in Fort Lauderdale. Back then our church had a morning service and an evening service. We always went to both.

There was nothing particularly special about this night in 1991. We didn't know that the guest speaker's words would change the direction of our life moving forward rather quickly. Dave had been working as an art director and design artist for a couple of years, but he felt something was missing. He was not fulfilled doing what he always thought he wanted to do. He had not really shared this with me yet. It was a struggle he was having in his own heart. We had been married almost three years at the time and on many occasions we had asked one another, "What do you think we'll do in the future?" We imagined a lot of things, but there was no clear path.

That night in his message, Danny DuVall said, "Are you doing everything you should be doing for God, or are you wasting your time and His?" This question hit Dave between the eyes and he pondered on it for a few moments. Danny then said, "If you are searching and wanting God to show you what you're really supposed to be doing in life, just ask Him, but be ready and willing to listen. Most people ask, but really don't want to know." After finishing his sermon, the preacher invited people that were searching for direction, to just stand where they were, close their eyes, and ask.

I didn't stand up. I was fine. I was working at a large law firm and had ascended from runner to receptionist to administrative assistant in a couple of years. I thought we were good and on our way to a little house with a white picket fence and a couple of babies. But Dave stood, put his hands up, and simply asked, "Ok, God, what am I supposed to be doing with my life?" He heard a voice inside that said, "Children's ministry and children's evangelism." He would tell me later that it was clear as day. Like a vision in his mind's eye, his artistic talents and things he loved to do suddenly all came together and made sense. He knew in that moment that God wanted him to use his abilities in acting, writing, and creating to reach children with the love of God.

There was a great secret God knew. Inside my husband lay hundreds of creative ideas and storylines that He had deposited in him. They were hidden inside of Dave waiting to be brought to life. Dave was not even aware of them yet. There was also great potential in me, but at the time, I didn't believe it.

I was sitting right next to him and had no idea all this was going on. I was oblivious to my young husband hearing the voice of God as he stood there asking and listening. I was oblivious to our future being shifted in those few moments.

As we were getting ready for bed that night, without much fanfare Dave proclaimed, "I know what we're supposed to be doing with our lives. Children's ministry and children's evangelism." I don't know if he was expecting me to jump up and down or what, but he certainly didn't get that. I just stared at him with a puzzled look. What? Work with kids? He must be joking. So my response was, "That must have not been God telling you that because I don't even like kids. I mean, I like my nephews and nieces and I know I'll love my own children, but I can't put up with other people's snotty-nosed brats." Then I added, "Look, I take a calling seriously. I'm not going to just grab my suitcases and go do something I am not sure I'm supposed to do just because. God has my mailbox, and if we're supposed to do this, He needs to let me know." Wow, yeah, that's what I said. Sassy. Just like that.

What was my super patient and wise husband's response? Dave said, "Okay, I get it. If this is God, and I know it is, He'll let you know too." With that, Dave just dropped the subject. He didn't say another word about it and silently prayed, "God get her."

Three months later, we were at another Sunday night church service. I went up to the altar for prayer because I had a migraine. To this day I don't know if I was healed or not, but I do remember what happened when I knelt at the altar. As I closed my eyes, waiting for the pastor to pray for me, I began to see children's faces. All kinds of children, from all races and backgrounds. They were afraid and crying. Some were hiding under beds and in closets because daddy was coming home drunk. Tears began to flow. God, what am I seeing? I thought. I heard the response inside my head, "They are the ones I am sending you to." "Why?" "Because you'll be able to relate to them and understand their broken hearts. You'll be able to reach them because of your own experiences." I cried and cried. I felt my heart break for these little ones. As my heart broke open, God was able to pour in the love that I needed for the children He was calling me to.

I came back to my seat and told Dave, "We need to go!" He thought I was literally saying we needed to leave to go home. He said, "Ok, grab your purse." I said, "No! I mean we need to go reach the children." Dave smiled. He realized God had dropped a love letter in my mailbox and it had changed my life. It was signed, sealed, and delivered. No question.

That night as I excitedly told Dave what I had experienced, he calmly walked over to the bedroom closet and pulled down a manila folder from the top shelf. Sneaky! He had hidden it there knowing I was too short to reach it!

Opening it, he began to show me sketches of a medieval castle stage, puppet designs, and the two of us in royal costumes. He had been in cahoots with God behind my back for the last three months. He said he was so sure that God would speak to me, that he felt it was wise to get prepared for when I was finally ready to listen. That was irritating for half a second. Then looking through his sketches, I said, "Ummm, no, I'm not wearing a costume, and I'm not speaking into a microphone. I don't know how to talk to kids! I was thinking my job would be to sit silently on the front row, praying and supporting you while you spoke."

I didn't realize that there was great potential in me to do everything that lay ahead for us if I'd just be willing to let God use me. I didn't believe I had much to offer for this "calling to children". I mean, Dave's talents were obvious and clear, but what could I bring to the kids' table? Dave answered me quickly and firmly, "No, we're doing this together. From now on we're a team. I am not going anywhere or doing anything without you. You'll be fine! You'll do great! We'll do it together."

That was the beginning of a great adventure and 26 years later, we'd still be "doing it together." It wasn't until many years after the "calling to reach children" while teaching children's ministry leaders in Iceland, that I received a revelation that added to this story.

As I was sharing my part of the testimony with the audience, I said, "In the beginning, I didn't even like kids." Immediately in my mind, I heard the words, "That's because you didn't like your own childhood." In a moment I realized that my earliest childhood memories were sad and full of fear. I abhorred my childhood and subconsciously I did not want to be reminded of all I had been through. So my answer was to just stay away from kids. Really, it wasn't that I didn't like kids, it was that I didn't like my own life as a kid. It wasn't until the night the Lord showed me the vision of the crying children that my spirit understood that my childhood pain had a purpose. He wastes nothing.

Once we agreed to say *YES* to what God was asking of us in 1991, we were all in!

We had no idea what the future would look like or the places this yes would take us, but we knew that it would be fun. This is when By Royal Decree Children's Ministry was born. Because of his background in advertising, Dave knew we needed to get pictures done and promote what we offered. In the weeks that followed, Dave designed and made our first puppets. He sketched out some costumes my mom sewed together for us. We dressed our nephew, Alfredo Andres (who we always called Andrew) in plastic pieces of armor and had him pose with us in a photo shoot. We had not done one service or event yet, but we sure did look the part in that homemade brochure! We mailed it out along with a cover letter introducing ourselves to hundreds of churches all over Florida as a start. Calls started coming in for bookings.

David & Jackie Smith

Eph 6:10-18

As soon as we had a few months scheduled, we quit our 9-to-5s and hit the road. That June we packed up our baby girl, handmade puppets, (which included the beloved Blu the Gorilla), costumes, and the castle set in our blue Toyota minivan and set off on a grand adventure. For two years we traveled full time going from church to church performing and ministering. Our entertaining and creative four-night events were embraced by so many who invited us back year after year. We shared the gospel with over 40,000 children and families our first year in full-time ministry. It was exciting and rewarding.

There are so many wonderful memories from those first years that I will treasure forever. People often said they had "never seen anything like it". Dave knew that if we could capture children's imaginations, we could earn the right to speak to their hearts. It became our great pleasure to share the love of Jesus in fun and creative ways.

Dave was all about creating whimsical, exciting adventures and experiences. Whether in ministry or at home with his own kids, he would be "all in" when having fun and creating an experience. He was not childish by any means, but he was truly childlike in his approach to life and ministry. My husband had a fun and delightful view on life. He so trusted his heavenly Father that he was able to easily sweep away cares and concentrate on what really mattered... living and enjoying life. He would always tell me, "Don't worry about it; God will take care of it."

That's exactly the kind of heart God wants us all to have, a trusting, childlike heart. This is possible and it is found in complete surrender and confidence in your heavenly Father. What's more like a child than living carefree and having all sorts of adventurous fun? What's more like a child than not worrying where Daddy will take them or how they'll get there? A child just sits back and enjoys the ride, knowing in their innermost being that Daddy has it handled. Jesus lovingly admonishes us, "Unless you become as a little child, you will not inherit the kingdom of heaven." My husband inherited the kingdom of heaven... too early for my liking. My Dave is now enjoying his heavenly reward. He is creating without limits, worshiping without restrictions and adventuring without boundaries!

David Smith heard a call in 1991 to dedicate his life to minister to children, then he heard another call in 2017 to "come Home." He faithfully answered both. I know His welcome home party was amazing, and when he ran into the arms of Jesus he heard the words we all long to hear, "Well done my good and faithful servant. Enter into the joy of your Lord." I can't wait to hear those words myself.

> *How can they call on him unless they believe in him?*
> *How can they believe in him unless they hear about him?*
> *How can they hear about him unless someone preaches to*
> *them? And how can anyone preach without being sent? It*
> *is written, 'How beautiful are the feet of those who bring*
> *good news!'*
>
> *—Romans 10:14-15 NIRV*

The Early Years

While attending the Art Institute of Fort Lauderdale from 1985 to 1987, David and I had become good friends. Because of his commitment not to date while in college, our friendship didn't develop into a romantic one until it was the right time. Looking back, I am thankful it worked out exactly that way. My impatience to start dating sooner could have ruined the solid foundation of friendship we ended up with.

During that all night telephone conversation, we decided that we would get married the following September. It was so easy to talk to someone who cared, understood and shared your dreams. It was so easy to dream about a fun future together. It was so easy to fall head over heals with David Smith. As the sun came up outside our windows, we both realized that life had just shifted and a new chapter had begun. I think I floated to my job that morning where I worked as a receptionist at a law office. I hadn't slept a wink all night, but it didn't matter.

One Wednesday night early in our dating relationship we sat at Burger King after church and talked about family—his, mine and the one we'd like to have some day. I remember that night distinctly because it felt like we were mapping out the journey ahead. It was another pivotal moment. We talked about our views on marriage, the shared responsibilities of a husband and wife, and how we would deal with challenges that would inevitably come along. We discussed how we would deal with and resolve conflicts and disagreements.

We talked a lot about family. His and mine. The lessons learned from our experiences growing up. He told me all about his siblings, John, Duane, and Dot, their spouses and their children. We were surprised to realize we each had seven nieces and nephews whom we absolutely adored. We agreed that God would be at the center of our marriage and that we didn't want to build a future without having Him leading us. These were the kinds of conversations that would solidify the foundation to build our future on.

My parents grew to love Dave as a son. Through the years I always joked that they loved him more than me. My father admired the way Dave treated me and I think secretly wished he could have been more like him. David's mother, Mary, was in my corner from day one and treated me like a daughter. Dave was always patient, kind, and thoughtful with the nephews and nieces on both sides of the family, which made my heart believe he would make a great father one day.

Our wedding day was the best day ever. The weather was perfect and everything went according to plan. I was so nervous and excited to marry my best friend. My father walked me to my waiting groom dressed in his white tux and tails. When asked, "Who gives this woman to be married to this man?" in broken English, my father was able to finally respond with the phrase he had been rehearsing for days, "Her mother and I do." It was a beautiful ceremony. After the pronouncement as husband and wife, Pastor Joe said, "You may kiss your bride." I think everyone was sort of shocked to see David lift my veil, lean in, and kiss me gently on the forehead.

Dave had already told me that this is what he would do. He explained that when his sister Dot married Rick, he saw his brother-in-law kiss his sister like that at the altar when he was just a little boy. This left such an impression on him of a sweet and romantic love, that this is how he always imagined kissing his bride at the altar. It meant something beautiful to us and it was another example of his intentional and thoughtful heart.

We had the nephews and nieces release red and white balloons into the gorgeous, blue Florida sky, and off we drove into our future. So hopeful, so full of dreams, and so in love.

Those first years of marriage were so much fun!

One morning in December of 1990, I woke up feeling really nauseous. A store-bought pregnancy test revealed that we were expecting our first child. We were so excited and just knew that this little one would bring so much joy to our home. In the following moths I gained a lot of weight… 58 pounds to be exact. I was at 40 weeks and our little girl was so comfortable in my womb that it seemed she didn't have any intention of coming out. I went in for an ultrasound on Monday, August 19, where they determined that she was perfectly healthy, but bigger than we imagined. My doctor explained that I was not dilating and if we waited any longer this baby could possibly weigh over 11 pounds! We would have to schedule a c-section for Wednesday. I was devastated because this is not how I imagined things would go. I cried all the way home and tried to wrap my brain around having to have surgery in two days. As we walked into our little apartment, the phone was ringing. I answered to my sister's voice saying, "Don't say anything. I was just praying for you and the Lord told me to tell you that you will need to have a cesarean because there may be complications otherwise. He said to tell you not to worry. Be at peace. This is part of His plan."

That was a miracle moment and I was so thankful that the Lord would send this message to me just in time. I was grateful for a sister that was praying and listening.

On August 21, 1991, our beautiful baby girl, Brittany Nicole, made her grand entrance. She was everything we dreamed of and more. They were right; this baby girl was big at 9 pounds and 12 ounces! Dr. Sarah, who was a short little lady, had to stand on a box to perform the surgery. At seeing our precious baby girl, she declared, "She's so big! You could put some books under her arm and send her to school!" What a fun time we had with her in those early years. Brittany was a funny, spunky, and sweet little doll and a "Daddy's girl" from day one.

"By Royal Decree Children's Ministry" was conceived and birthed right around the same time Brittany was. In June of 1992, we packed up our van with puppets, costumes and a castle set. Brittany was just 10 months old when she took her first steps at a church in Clarksville, Tennessee. We traveled full time for 2 years sharing the love of Jesus with thousands of kids and families all over the east coast. Feeling the desire to settle down a bit, we accepted our first children's pastors position at a church in Boca Raton, Florida.

Soon after, we were expecting again. It was a hot, South Florida August day in 1994 when we met our first son, David Alexander. This chunky, blue-eyed ten-pounder stole our hearts from the first moment we laid eyes on him. But God was not done blessing us... Six months after welcoming baby number two, we were surprised to find out we were expecting baby number three! We were not planning on getting pregnant so soon. I remember breaking the news to my husband by saying, "Do you believe God is faithful?" It might sound like an odd way to tell your spouse you're pregnant, but we were struggling financially and I was not looking forward to having a third c-section. Dave's quick and certain answer was, "Of course I believe God is faithful!"

"Well, I'm pregnant."

Dave just laughed and hugged me and that was that.

I prayed that this precious one would "look like my side of the family" and the Lord answered my prayer. Jonathan (Jonny) William arrived two weeks early at a whopping 9 pounds, 6 ounces. This handsome brown-eyed, brown-haired smiley boy was the perfect addition to our little family. Within four and half years we became a family of five and we couldn't have been happier.

We began getting restless and missed being on the road. Dave and I agreed that we were the most fulfilled when we were traveling and sharing the Word of God in creative ways through our themed events. I began booking places to minister and was surprised at how quickly our calendar filled up. So when Jonny was just seven months old we decided to put all our belongings in a storage unit, pack up our three little ones, and go on the road once again. Another year on the road this time with three kids under five years of age was challenging, yet they were the most fun. Those days on the road when it was just the five of us, hold the sweetest memories for me.

A new opportunity came our way in 1997. Again ready to settle down and have a "home," we accepted the invitation to be the children's pastors at North Georgia Worship Center. The thought of moving away from our family in South Florida was hard, but we were excited for the next adventure. Our three years in Gainesville, Georgia, hold a lot more bittersweet memories. It was in those years where we found an even deeper relationship with the Lord. As the summer of 2000 approached, Dave and I began to feel a familiar restlessness in our spirit. We knew that our time there was coming to an end.

Our next big move would happen in July of 2000. God clearly led us to Huntsville, Alabama. We embraced "The Rocket City" and made it our home to this day. Dave and I faithfully served as the children's pastors over the elementary age ministry at The Rock Family Worship Center for seventeen years. All in all we were in full time children's ministry for twenty-six years. Dedicating ourselves to instilling God's love in little one's hearts and staying the course for that long is something I am proud of. It is an experience I will never regret.

Dave and I were fortunate to do a lot of wonderful things in our 30 plus years together, but our greatest accomplishment was and will always be our three children. What an honor it has been to be Brittany, David and Jonathan's mom and dad! They are our greatest creative collaboration!

Looking back at all those years of marriage, raising a family and ministry, from beginning to end, I can smile with contentment knowing we were faithful to God and always wanted to follow His will. Our life together was really great. Was it perfect? No. If I could go back in time, I would definitely do some things differently. But we can't park ourselves in the regrets. That will get us nowhere.

The following quote became our children's ministry motto and today it reminds me to look back with a smile and continue moving forward with faith.

May we never ever stop…

*"Learning from the past,
as we quest to the future!"*

Purpose-full Departure

L eading up to November 2017 we kept busy with family, church, ministry, work, and our fairly new business, Wow Parties.

The church where we served as children's pastors for 17 years, The Rock Family Worship Center, was moving to a new location and there was a lot going on. The Rock had purchased a huge building, formerly Butler High School. In July 2000 we came on staff as the lead children's pastors when there were only about 400 members and 50 kids. Our church grew progressively bigger and bigger as a congregation, adding four additional campuses as the years went on. Loving and serving the city of Huntsville, Alabama and surrounding areas had become a part of who we were. Finally moving to this new facility was something we had all been waiting and praying many years for. The dream and the possibilities this new building held for us in reaching and teaching even more children were wonderful and we were excited. Dave was super excited!

By mid-November, the daunting move from the building we had been in for fifteen years had already begun. The great collection and accumulation of costumes, props, curriculum, puppets, and all kinds of other children's ministry stuff from the huge attic had already been packed and moved to the new building on Holmes Avenue.

There was still so much to do. We had been planning and dreaming up what the new children's ministry auditorium and other rooms would look like. Dave imagined, sketched out, and dreamed up a great design for the stage. It would be a bigger and better, updated steampunk-themed time machine, stage, and set. He worked with the architects and builders on design ideas and what would work and wouldn't. He had promised the children a beautiful new "Kids Quest" sanctuary to worship and learn in. Dave was determined to deliver. We made lists on items to purchase and build. We even tried to figure out where the two-story slide would go.

Dave had already begun to set up what he planned would be his workshop, the "Creation Station." This was the first room we cleaned out and painted together at Butler High School in preparation for the plans he had. Dave's dream was to have a workshop to build sets, work on props, and make one of a kind puppets. This dream included teaching others building and painting techniques and passing on his knowledge. The possibilities were endless on what he could create and teach others in that space. Dave was generous in sharing anything he knew about creativity and design.

That week in November we were also working on another dream, the "Holiday House" at Big Spring Park in downtown Huntsville. This would be a place where kids and families could come visit and have fun holiday pictures made with their favorite princess and hero characters throughout the season. We invested in the purchase of the little Holiday House and began working on making it a Christmas experience right next to the Museum of Art. This was just one of the many creative ideas we had for the businesses we would launch in the coming years.

Since stepping out of my paid position at the church a couple of years prior, I had been working with one of my best friends and business partner, Teri, on starting up a business that had also been a 20-year dream for Dave and me. Teri and her husband, Jeff had become close friends and like family over the years. They truly believed in us and our creative ideas. Together we started Dui Corp. as the covering for Wow Parties. We came to find out by accident one day playing Scrabble that the word Dui means "double duo," which we immediately agreed symbolized the four of us. Wow Parties began with providing fun character visits for parties and events and had grown into mascot management for our local hockey team and themed party planning and decorating.

Dave and I dreamt of owning a beautiful building that would house creative and amazing themed party rooms for kids. This was the big idea that had been in the works in our hearts and minds for all these years. We thought that it would be a great way to continue to serve children and families as we made a living after stepping out of full-time children's ministry one day. We realized we could not be "relatable, cool children's pastors" in our grey-haired years and that others needed to take on the mantle. We knew at some point soon, we'd pass on the baton to others to run with. We desired to continue to pour into and train children's pastors and ministers as we grew older. We felt we would be over children's ministry eventually and not in it.

Dave would say, "When we were young, we were the cool children's pastors, then we became the cool aunt and uncle, then more like the cool parents, but I cannot be a grandpa children's pastor; that's not cool anymore. When I'm of age to be a grandfather, I won't be serving in this capacity any longer." We had no idea how prophetic these words were! We had worked and ministered side by side reaching thousands of children with the love of Jesus for 26 years. We were on staff at The Rock for over 17 years. I worked in the office with Dave since day one. Even after I stepped down from my paid office position at the church, I continued to work with Dave on Sundays, teaching leadership classes and writing curriculum. This was a huge part of our lives.

We wrote, planned, and executed anything and everything having to do with the elementary-age children's ministry together. We worked on staff at this church side by side, teaching kids every Sunday morning about God's love in creative ways. We had the privilege of raising hundreds of leaders that served with us in so many capacities. The previous 17 years had been an adventure we loved living together. Ministry was part of our love story. We always loved creating, writing, working, and ministering together. Life was always busy for us. We were always doing something, and this last season of his life was no different.

November 23, 2017 was a beautiful Thanksgiving Day. Most of the family gathered in our home as had become tradition. After everyone left that evening, Dave helped me clean up. I'll never forget leaning up against the kitchen island next to him. I reached over, put my arms around his waist, laid my head on his chest and hugged him tightly. I whispered a very sincere, "Thank you." He shrugged and said, "What for?" This was his usual answer, not wanting any recognition for being amazing. With my arms still around him, I answered, "For helping me clean up. You're awesome." I believe we kissed. I wish with all my heart I could remember.

We went back into our bedroom and began getting ready for bed. As I reflected on the day, it dawned on me that we had hardly taken any pictures. This was so out of the ordinary for me. I normally take dozens of pictures of any family gathering, no matter how small. As I checked my phone I realized that only two pictures had been taken this Thanksgiving Day. The first picture was of my three children holding Jonny's birthday cake and the other, interestingly enough, was of the whole family who was gathered that day… except Dave. My husband hardly ever took photos. That was always my thing. But on this day, as we were about to overload our plates with the feast before us, Dave turned around and said, "Everyone get together and let me take a picture." This was spontaneous and a little out of character for him, so it stood out to me.

As I climbed in bed that night, I was aggravated about not having more pictures to remember this Thanksgiving by. As I opened up the photos on my phone and looked at the only two pictures from that day, I sighed dramatically and said, "Babe! I can't believe we only took two pictures today!" He had been in the bathroom getting ready for bed. He walked over to my side of the bed, leaned over close to me, and looked at the pictures. Then I said, "And you're not even in this one! You should've selfied yourself in." Of course, my Dave never thought to "selfie" himself into any picture. That's just the way he was, selfless. But now I feel like it was another foretelling moment in time where God was giving us yet another clue as to what was about to

happen. In this last picture of Thanksgiving 2017, the family is gathered around me as I stood in the middle of the group... without Dave by my side. He was not in the picture.

As I complained about the lack of photos taken that day, Dave came in close to me to look at the picture he took and I will never forget what he did and said next. With his two fingers he expanded the image on my phone, making me the largest and central part on the screen. He then said, "But look at you. Look how cute you are. You're so cute." Those sweet words will forever be seared in my memory, as they were the last few I would ever hear him utter in this life…. and that would be the last time I saw his precious face while alive. Dave then walked into the bathroom. I called out from the bed, "Honey, you've had a long day, come to bed." From the bathroom, he said, "I'm going to wash the mascot costume tonight, before tomorrow's game." Lazily I said, "Can't we just do that in the morning? The game is not until 3:00." His response was, "Let me at least get it into the dryer so we don't have to worry about it tomorrow."

Our last words to each other were…

Me, "Do you want me to help you?" and his response was, "No, I got it."

I fell asleep. It was around midnight.

My biggest regret is…I don't remember if we kissed goodnight.

The kids and I have tried to piece together and imagine what might have happened after I fell asleep. We know now that our son David saw his dad after he returned from Black Friday shopping around 1:30 in the morning. Dave was in the kitchen standing with his back up against one of the counters and was looking at his phone. I'm guessing he was playing his Star Wars game, waiting on the costume to finish drying and for David to come home. David said they talked for a few minutes about his purchases and then said their final words to each other.

"Good night, Bub, love you." "Good night Dad, love you too. See you in the morning."

"See you in the morning, son." David said that he looked back over his shoulder as he walked down the hallway towards his room and saw his dad doing what he normally did every night at the end of the day, locking the doors and turning off lights. Nothing seemed out of the ordinary.

At 3:25 AM, I was awakened out of a deep sleep by two sounds I will never forget.

The first sound was like none other I have ever heard. It was a deep, loud "whooph."

It's hard for me to describe it in our human language. This was a sound I can only describe as a huge suction mixed with a deep swoosh. It was "otherworldly." This was immediately followed by a loud crash, which I would soon realize was Dave's body and head hitting the tile bathroom floor.

These two intense back-to-back sounds woke me from a deep sleep, Whooph! BAM!

In a sweeping motion and all at once, I sat up and threw the cover off of me knowing in my deepest being that I had just heard something that was monumental and would change my life forever. It didn't take but two seconds for me to get to him. The bathroom door was open and the overhead light was on. My Dave was lying on his back on the bathroom floor.

Our new puppy had somehow gotten to him before I did and was licking his face. I pushed her aside, knelt close to him, and began to say, "Sweetheart, sweetheart, what happened?" My first shocked thought was that he had slipped and knocked himself out.

I'll never forget those agonizing moments! My desperation of not knowing what to do or what was happening. His eyes were closed and he was pale. His left arm slightly contracted involuntarily. Immediately I realized, and I don't know how, that it was his heart. I said, "Babe, no, no! I love you! You're my sweetheart! You're the love of my life!" I knew it was bad. I screamed at the top of my lungs to God in desperation, "No, no, no! Oh, God no, please! No! He's my sweetheart!" I ran to wake up my son. I threw open David's bedroom door and screamed "Call 911, I think Daddy's had a heart attack!"

David jumped out of bed and called the emergency number all at once as he ran to his father. David told them, "I think my dad's had a heart attack," gave them our address, and began to perform CPR following the direction of the woman on the other end of the phone. "One, two three, four, you're doing good. One, two, three, four, stay calm."

I ran in circles. I prayed. I screamed for help. I cried. I ran to wake my mother and asked her to pray. I ran back and forth begging God not to take him as David continued with the CPR.

"One, two, three, four."

I kept saying, "I don't know what to do! God, he's my sweetheart. The love of my life!"

In between chest compressions and with the phone being held by his shoulder, David screamed at me, "Mom, call people to pray!" I grabbed my cell phone and began dialing numbers. I don't recall who I called or what I said. I didn't know what I was supposed to do. I was experiencing something completely foreign to me. This was a moment I had never rehearsed or prepared for.

I ran out the front door, screaming into the cold night air. I screamed for help. I screamed to the heavens, "God! No!! Please no!" I remember it was very cold, the sky was black and dotted with hundreds of beautiful twinkling stars.

The neighborhood was eerily, completely quiet, and still.

Everything and everyone was still.

I was out of control.

I pounded on my neighbor's door in what felt was an eternity, but everyone was asleep.

I screamed at the starry sky again hoping for a miraculous answer to my desperation.

It felt like no one could hear my desperate, gut-wrenching cries for help.

It all felt like I was in a slow-motion nightmare where you desperately beg and cry for help and no one hears you. This whole time, David stayed with his dad, doing everything he could. Living his own nightmare.

Finally, paramedics showed up. My thoughts were like a rapid-fire machine gun in my mind... They're too calm. They're not moving fast enough. Don't they know this is my whole life? This is the love of my life! Do something. Anything. Please God, don't take him.

Now they're not letting me in the room. The police officer is asking me to calm down and I'm screaming at him, "You don't understand, that's my sweetheart. He's the love of my life! Please, please help him!" How can they ask me to calm down? They have me turn around while they take him out to the ambulance. Why???

In the midst of this, our neighbors run in and try to console us. Clay says he'll drive us to the hospital. We will follow the ambulance. I run to put on some shoes and find my coat. As we get in Clay's car, I realize the ambulance is still there. Why have they not left?

We pull out behind the ambulance, but they are not speeding. The emergency lights are not on. In desperation, in confusion, and pain, I'm wailing, but the siren on the ambulance is not. Why?! Maybe he's woken up and he's going to be ok, that's why they're not rushing...or maybe they know he's gone and they can't do anything else? Dear God, no! My thoughts were everywhere.

Someone told me I made more phone calls as we drove, but I just don't remember. In the emergency room, I begged the nurse to tell me how he was and her reply was, "They're doing everything they can." This is not an answer I wanted! I wanted to hear "He is fine," "He will be fine."

They took me, my mother, and my pastors into the tiny waiting room that I now know is reserved for those that are probably awaiting the most horrible news they've ever gotten about their loved one. My brother joined us as we waited to hear what would happen.

David had gone to get his brother and we had already gotten in contact with Brittany and knew she was on her way from Nashville.

The next hour felt like an eternity waiting on Seth to drive Brittany to me and for Jonny to join us. I just wanted my kids with me. I needed them with me. All I could do was pray and pace. I couldn't stop shaking. I remember saying over and over again, "God, I still trust you. God, you're still good."

Finally, a nurse came in and said the words no wife who's married to the greatest husband on earth wants to hear, ***"I'm sorry, Mrs. Smith. Your husband has passed away."***

I screamed through my tears, "God I still trust you!" In that moment I had to say it out loud and choose not to take it back.

Then a million thoughts began to ricochet through my mind.

Purpose-full Departure

This can't be happening.

We were just together enjoying life and each other.

We had just had a great Thanksgiving Day.

What do you mean he's gone?

How?

Why?

He wasn't sick.

He's only 50.

We were just starting to have so much fun.

We have plans.   Dreams.

Grandchildren will be coming soon.

We've picked out the pirate ship bed

they will sleep in one day.

We were going to have more adventures.

This can't be real life.

Not now.

We were supposed to grow old together.

What is happening?

Now I'm in a fog.

A dense fog.

I don't know if I'm awake or dreaming.

Maybe it's both. It's a living nightmare.

By this time Brittany, David and Jonny are with me. I had to tell them. My amazing kids are strong, but right now they have crumbled into each other's arms and are distraught. We held each other and wept bitterly. What else could we do?

They offered us the opportunity to see him one more time. Together we locked arms and walked down the hallway and through the heavy double doors. One of the hardest decisions we've ever had to make. One that will live on, etched in our hearts and minds forever.

We were able to see him, touch him, talk to him. Tell him what we wanted to say. I gave him as many kisses as I possibly could and it just wasn't enough.

My hero and knight in shining armor was gone.

My dear, sweet, loving man, just lying there... lifeless...was too much to take in, but we stood and loved him together as a family one last time, "the original five" as the kids would often say when it was just us. Seth, Heather, and Rachel joined us in our solemn goodbyes. My mother was able to say goodbye as well. She loved him like a son. He loved her too.

We had a chance to spend time with him and say our final goodbyes.

All I could breathe out was, "See you soon, my love."

And a final kiss.

I hated leaving him there. I didn't want to go. Even in this dense murky reality, I knew this was only his body, an empty shell now. But, I loved that body. Every single part was mine, as I was his. We had aged together in the last 30 years, but we still only had eyes for each other, so walking away from his physical body was so very hard. The real David William Smith was now more alive than I could even comprehend.

The next few days are like a foggy memory. I had to will myself to breathe. I don't know how the kids and I survived but for the grace and mercy of God. Our whole family had been shaken, and we'd never be the same again.

My children and I have felt and believed from the very beginning of this grief-filled journey that Dave had a supernatural encounter in those early morning hours. There were some interesting things about Dave's last hours that we began to piece together and ponder on as the next few days gave way to thinking about what might have taken place. I had to process what I heard for a couple of days amid the most intense grief of my life. The sound that woke me. What did I hear? It wasn't a groan or struggled call for help. It was such a strange sound…and the fall. By the sound of the fall and the way he fell, straight back in what God would later tell me was a "trust fall," he should've cracked his head open on that cold, hard tile floor, but he didn't.

In reflecting on the way everything happened, we began to see God's orchestration of it all. One or two things would be a coincidence, but all of these things together make us believe that this was a God-ordained moment for our favorite man. These are things that cannot be explained and we have thought and talked about ever since that day.

First, the sound that woke me up was not normal. Other than

the second sound, which was his body hitting the floor, there were no other sounds such as a struggle to breathe or a call for help. Only a great whoosh and the crash of his fall. I came to find out a couple of days later that someone had asked the nurse in the hospital that night, "Do you think he suffered?" and she answered, "Oh, no, sir! He was gone before he hit the ground." That was a confirmation of the sound I heard. I knew in this moment that God allowed me to hear him leave his body!

Later we realized that nothing in the bathroom was out of place. All the doors connected to the bathroom were closed, including closets and toilet area, except the one that was open to our bedroom. This is strange because normally, if Dave was in the bathroom, especially with the overhead light on, he would have closed the door to not wake me. But the overhead light was on and the door to our bedroom wide open. If that door had not been open I would not have been able to get to him because he would have fallen behind it.

Dave had taken his glasses off and set them down on the bathroom counter, which is also strange because he normally would have done this right before getting in bed. His cell phone was turned off and sitting by the sink as well. This was also out of the ordinary, as plugging it in at his nightstand to charge was also one of the last things he would do.

According to where he was lying when I found him, he would have been standing about two feet from the closet door. There is no reason as to why he would just be standing there. He was not facing either of the two sinks or mirror. If he had been, he would have fallen back into the bathtub. He fell supine in the only place that a 6-foot-tall man could have lain as if sleeping. He fell straight back and did not hit a wall or even the one open door.

There was no indication that he was washing his face or brushing his teeth. There was no indication that he was doing anything except just standing facing his closed closet door. I know this because a couple of days after his passing I lay on the tile floor placing my head where his was when I found him. I then counted six 1-foot tiles to determine where he had been standing when he fell backward. I stood there for a while, still in shock and whispered, "Sweetheart, what did you see? What was the last thing on your mind? I wish I could see what you saw." My eyes went directly to the wall to the right of his closet door. The only words in that bathroom are on a small sign he hung there months before. It says, "I love you more." Of course, you did.

When I first found Dave on the floor, both his arms were at his side and there was absolutely no sign of struggle or pain. He looked like he had laid himself down flat on his back. The very last thing he had always done before getting in bed all our married life was to take off his t-shirt. This is how I know he never came to bed that night. When I got to him he still had his t-shirt on. He was wearing a grey t-shirt and grey boxers. Remembering this a few days later, the boys and I looked up the meaning of the color grey. Grey means death, but it also means "humility and painlessness." Another message from the Lord that would confirm that he did not suffer at all.

Later, we were surprised to learn that the hospital emergency room where my sweetheart was last in repose and where we said our final goodbyes was room number fourteen. In ancient Jewish numerology, fourteen is the numeric value of the name David! God showed me through this that even the hospital room my husband was last in, was ordained and on purpose.

We believe with all of our hearts that in those final moments on earth, Dave saw the veil between the two realms part. His eyes were opened to the Kingdom he longed for. I imagine that the brilliant light, amazing fragrances, and extraordinary colors were glorious! I know in that moment he saw his guardian angels standing beside him. I believe they were the two he sketched out long ago, "Rejoice" and "Guardian". Jesus Himself might have arrived to take His son home. For just a split second Dave may have thought of us, as he heard the Lord say, "Son, it's your time. You can stay and continue to do good things or come with Me and they will do great things." I imagine Dave turning back at the One he loved most with a huge smile on his face saying, "Let's do this." Jesus surely said, "Well done my good and faithful servant, enter into the joy of your Lord." With that, I can see my Dave planting his feet like Superman as he always told the kids he would do, and looking into eternity, he shot through the atmosphere with a whoosh leaving his outer shell to fall to the ground. It was the sound of that earthly departure that woke me.

This amazing husband of mine, the love of my life, got his greatest wish in that moment, to race through the galaxy with Jesus and His angels. I don't blame him for not choosing to stay. I think that once you've caught a glimpse of the Eternal One, there's nothing that compares.

Right now, my beloved Dave is worshiping His Creator, planning all the adventures we will have, and building beautiful things for our mansions. One day I will step through that veil and there will be a beautiful reunion! We will run to Jesus together and never have to say goodbye again.

As water reflects the face,

so one's life reflects the heart.

The Most Giving Heartbeat

S ince day one, I slept to the right side of Dave and he to my left. Whether we were home, in a hotel, or as guests in someone's home, that's the way it always was.

The bed.

Our bed.

Always a sanctuary.

A place of rest, love, intimacy, prayer, and security.

There we would often lie and Dave would say, "This. No one else has this. This is ours alone." Meaning that we were and only had been for each other since day one.

He would often add, "As long as we have this, we'll be okay." I would snuggle up against him. He would slip his right arm underneath me and bring me in close. I'd put my head on his chest and my right hand on his heart. Intentionally listening to his heartbeat, I would purposefully take in the warmth of his body and tune in to his breathing in the silence of the room. He'd reach over with his left hand and place it over mine. We'd lay there like that, quietly. I could hear the beating of his heart, the pulsing lifeblood running through his veins. It's crazy, but I must confess that many times I wondered in my mind, What would I ever do if this heart stopped beating? I would not be able to go on. How would mine ever beat again? I could never live without him." I would quickly shake off those thoughts with my next thought, That's crazy; we have too much life to live, too many dreams yet to accomplish, too many things to do for God.

I would have never thought that he was done here on earth and that those fleeting thoughts would become a reality much too soon.

He was only 50. When I was little, 50 was "old"! I remember thinking that anyone that was over 50 was really old. In my mind, that was the age of grannies and people with canes. But now I realize it's actually the age when you really start living.

We were in a really good place. Blessed with three grown children who had turned out to be amazing humans. These kids could now work and take care of themselves. They had each found the love of their life. We were finally at an age to really pour into the next generation and allow them to build on the foundation we had laid out. Our desire was to allow them to step up as we stepped forward to do other things. At our age, we figured this was the time to step into being over ministry, concentrating on teaching others how to do what we had done for so long.

Now at 50, we were confident in who we were and could begin making plans for the next season of life which involved doing the things we set aside while we were raising the kids and building a ministry. We would begin a new season where the business ideas we held on to for many years could possibly be birthed.

We were at a place where we were content and relaxed and secure in our relationships with others. We had learned to weed out the negative people who could bring us down and enjoy lifelong friends we would take vacations and cruises with.

Dave wasn't sick. He hardly ever got sick. Sure, he had some issues with high blood pressure, but he was exercising and had lost weight. He was feeling great. He looked great!

My husband's last 24 hours were filled with everything he loved. His heart was full. He was content. He had a long lunch with our son David the day before. He had been busy working on projects he loved. We laughed, joked, and had good conversations with our daughter Brittany as he basted the turkey with that garlic-injection thingy that he was so excited about. He helped me prepare and clean the house for guests on Thanksgiving Day. We enjoyed the usual feast with the family, and he had a second helping of dessert. He took the expected Thanksgiving afternoon nap in the recliner. Later in the evening, he was the handler for Chaos at the Huntsville Havoc game, spending quality time with our son Jonny. When he came home from the game, he jumped in and played games with our nieces and nephews. We laughed so much through a few competitive rounds of Pictionary. Afterward, I remember he sat and showed some of the family videos of a fellow creative he admired so much, Bruce Barry, and the work he was doing for Disney hotels. He was so excited about that project and said he would love to get to see it one day.

When everyone had finally left, some headed home and others to do some Black Friday shopping, Dave and I found ourselves alone in the kitchen. As always, he helped me clean up and put dishes in the dishwasher. After wiping down the counters, we rested together against the kitchen island, and I hugged him tightly. I said, "Thank you babe, you're awesome." God, I'm so glad I have that memory of saying "Thank you" one last time. I had so much to be thankful for on that Thanksgiving night. He was and will always be such a blessing to me and I feel like I didn't give him enough "thank yous".

Thanksgiving was probably his favorite holiday, to be honest. He loved Christmas, but Thanksgiving was actually the beginning of the Christmas season for us. This is when the weather really starts changing and family and friends begin gathering for all kinds of celebrations. This is the time of year we would get serious about making sure we had our gift-giving lists for the kids planned out and all kinds of secret, fun plans would be made to make things special for our family.

Traditionally, on the day after Thanksgiving, we put away all the fall decor first thing in the morning. There was a system and an order in our home for decorating for holidays. Everyone that knew Dave knew he had an issue with decorating for Christmas before Thanksgiving. Anyone who put up their Christmas tree or lights before Thanksgiving would be declared an "Eggnog." He would say, "Each holiday needs to have its own time of celebration and attention. Why do people get in a hurry to decorate for Christmas when Thanksgiving isn't even here yet? Everything has a time."

So, on the day after Thanksgiving each year, after the fall decor was packed up, then, and only then, would Dave begin bringing down box after box of Christmas treasures from the attic. Hundreds of memories stored carefully in red and green plastic boxes. Each box contained festive Christmas decorations and collections. My snowmen and mangers. His Christmas Story and Captain America themed trees. We had now accumulated over a dozen trees small and great that would be put up in all the available spots all over the house.

Our favorite thing, which we would always save for last, was the big family tree that would normally go in the den. This tree was always the one to be the keeper of all the very special ornaments collected since our very first Christmas as newlyweds. This tree was given the most attention and care because it was a symbol of our family. Dave took great care to make sure all the lights were working, and then we'd put on the Hallmark Channel with their endless, cheesy Christmas movies as a backdrop, grab a snack and begin decorating. The very last detail was putting the star at the very top of the tree.

Our tradition for all of Brittany's life was for her Daddy to pick her up and let her put the star on the very top. This sweet tradition continued each year. Even when Britt moved out of the house, the tree would be decorated, but the star would not go on the tree until she came home.

On this tree, you can find all kinds of ornaments that have special meaning to our family. From rocking horses, skateboards, puppies, ballerinas, to cell phones, superheroes, and macaroni art from school, all on familiar silver hooks. We added decorative red and gold ball ornaments as "fillers" as my husband called them because "There should be no open spots in between the branches." This tree was finished off with gold sparkly ribbon. Dave was into every detail and made sure that even our tree was displayed in excellence. Not for anyone else, but just for us to enjoy.

Throughout the years we gave each other and our children a special ornament each year that symbolized something they enjoyed or a significant event in their life from the previous year. We gave the kids their new ornament to open either on Christmas Eve or Christmas morning.

In October of 2017, just one month before he passed, Dave said, "Hey, let's start a new tradition this year. Let's give each other our special ornaments for the year on Thanksgiving instead of Christmas so that way as the kids begin their new lives in their own homes, they can put it right on their tree when they decorate right after Thanksgiving. This way they can enjoy it all season instead of waiting a whole year to hang it on the tree." I said, "Honey, that's a great idea…why didn't we think to do this before?" So, true to form, always planning ahead, he promptly began looking for the ornaments that would be significant to our kids that year. Brittany had just auditioned and gotten her golden ticket for American Idol, so he found on eBay the one and only American Idol ornament they had ever made. When we got it in the mail a few days later, we realized you could record something on it, so he found Brittany actually singing the song she auditioned with and we recorded it on the ornament. For David, he had already purchased the annual tradition: the new Hallmark guitar ornament for 2017. Since David began to play years ago, we always got him that year's design. Jonny and Rachel had just gotten engaged at Beast's Castle at Disney World, so of course we had to get them the Beauty and the Beast ornament with the rose in the dome, just like how her ring was presented to her in August.

Dave was the best gift giver! He planned ahead, made purchases, hid the gifts, and wrapped them himself. Of course, I was a part of the planning, purchasing and wrapping for the kids, but he was great at planning and keeping surprises for me. Although I love to receive gifts, they are not my love language. I love to give gifts because it makes the recipient happy, but I'm not a plan-ahead kind of gift giver. I'm usually running around at the last minute putting something together. I joked that he "one-upped" me all the time when it came to his thoughtful gift-giving.

Two times in particular stand out to me as some of the most unique and thoughtful gifts Dave ever gave me. In the weeks leading up to Christmas 2009, Dave kept sneaking away to the garage each evening. I remember getting annoyed with him a couple of times. After looking for him around the house, I would step out into the garage and say, "Honey, what are you doing?" He always responded with, "Oh, nothing just working on something." It did not occur to me that he was diligently and meticulously working on a gift for me. On Christmas morning I was very surprised to unwrap an action figure... of me!

Dave had taken parts and pieces of various action figures and put them together to make a Jackie doll! Who does this? The miniature me came complete with some items I used in real life; a Bible, a Scrabble game and a microphone. The little me-doll even had a replica of my button down Kids Quest shirt and black high heels. He extended the original doll's hair using hot glue and painted it to look like mine. The packaging was all hand made as well. So amazing and so thoughtful!

On a few occasions in our marriage, Dave and I reminisced about our favorite childhood toys. I told him the story about how as a little girl, some of my dolls and toys had come from discard piles. I explained that in the early days in the United States my parents learned that people in the "rich neighborhoods" often threw out really nice things for trash collection day. As the saying goes, "one man's trash is another man's treasure". We would often drive around those neighborhoods the night before trash pick up day and see what we could find.

One of my favorite finds was a movable, plastic cowgirl doll.

I loved this blond haired, blue bodied cowgirl doll and played with her all the time. I mentioned to him how much I regretted that even though this doll probably came with many accessories, I had only found a couple of pieces with her in the trash. At some point I lost that doll in our move to Florida around the age of ten.

On Christmas morning 2015 I was overcome with emotion and broke out in tears when I opened a beautifully wrapped box to find her, Jane West! There she was, the long lost doll from my childhood in her original box… with all her accessories! The little hand written note inside said, "Because you deserve all the pieces".

What a wonderful surprise. What a wonderful man.

Always going above and beyond. Somehow giving me what I didn't know I needed.

His last Thanksgiving was no exception…

After we had eaten lunch and the rest of the family had sort of dispersed to chat, grab coffee and desserts, and begin the first round of "Chicken Leg," Dave and I found ourselves sitting on the couch alone. I looked over at the small table by the wall and was pleasantly surprised to see four beautiful, little gold gift bags in a row. I nodded over at the unexpected bundles and whispered to Dave, "Are those the ornaments for the kids?" With a sweet smile, he answered, "Yes." Of course, in my Thanksgiving Day busyness, I had forgotten all about the ornaments, but he had not. Not only did he remember them, but he had also wrapped them and labeled each one with the recipient's name on a little tag. I smiled back and mouthed, "Thank you."

We noticed that no one was sitting at the dining room table, which was unusual with a house full of people. We thought this was a great opportunity to sit with our three kids and tell them about the new tradition by giving them their ornaments. I asked our kids to gather at the dining room table for something special. Jonny had Rachel on the phone since she had gone out of town with her family.

As we sat down, Dave proceeded to say, "Mommy and I decided to start a new tradition this year. From now on we're going to give you your Christmas ornaments on Thanksgiving so you can put them on your tree when you decorate in your own homes." He handed out a gift bag to each of our kids and one to me! I didn't expect he'd have one for me. I said, "But I haven't gotten yours yet!" He just smiled.

The kids opened their gifts and thanked us. I opened mine last and it was as thoughtful as expected and also foretelling. My ornament was a cute little Minnie Mouse holding a gift bag that read "Girl's best friend." In her tiny gift bag was a puppy which symbolized the pup we had just gotten in August. We had no clue in those blissful moments that just a few hours later my best friend in the world would be leaving for eternity and my sweet puppy, Renaissance Belle, would become my new best companion.

On his last day on earth, my Dave gave thanks to God,

bestowed gifts on his family, laughed and played, ate good food, and loved us so well. If he had been asked, "What would you like for your last day on earth to look like?" he would have described this exact day.

Dave's heartbeat was for his God and his family. Even now, in the silence of the night, when I find myself alone in our bed, I can close my eyes and hear his heart beating for us, loving us still. The sweetest heart I've ever known.

As water reflects the face, so one's life reflects the heart.

—*Proverbs 27:19 NIV*

Words of Life

———— ✦〰〰◦ ————

rief is a deep, lonely place. It cannot be explained. Sometimes it's what I imagine drowning would feel like. In the days that followed Dave's passing, I wasn't sure if I could face another day. How would I live? How would I function, stand, eat, talk? I didn't want to do any of that. What now?

I don't know.   I am numb.   I can't think.   I can't breathe.   He's gone?   Forever from this earth?   It can't be. This can't be happening to me.   To us.

These were my thoughts as I stepped into the bathroom to get ready for the day. It had only been five days since he flew away. Five days too many.

I had to somehow get myself together because I needed to take my best friend to the airport. Regina had flown in from Texas immediately to my side when she heard the news. She and Nelson were our best friends of 32 years. They proved it by showing up when I needed them the most. Nelson had spoken some of the sweetest words a best friend could speak at Dave's home-going celebration just two days before. He honored his "pal" with familiar stories and heartfelt words. I was so thankful they were with me for these five days. Today, they had to head back. The thought of them leaving was another gray cloud to add to my foggy, dark sadness.

I needed to brush my hair, put on real clothes and try to function. As I started to get ready, it felt like I was walking through invisible jello. All I could think of was "He's gone." All I wanted was to be held by my husband, but he was gone. I was distraught as I opened his walk-in closet door and stepped inside. I could smell him. His scent. I fell into his empty button-down shirts and wept. Bitterly.

In anguish, I screamed silent screams into these familiar, empty pieces of clothing. "Babe, I don't think I can do this without you! I don't know how I'm going to live another day. I just can't do this." Suddenly, something caught my eye. On the floor, in the corner of his closet was a long, rectangular box. It was opened on one end as if inviting me to look inside. Through tears, I thought, "What is that?" I had never seen or noticed it before. The label on the outside was marked UPS and the date was 2013. I picked up the box and pulled out a large, rolled up paper with a wall decal on it. I unrolled the paper and read the words, "You are stronger than you seem, braver than you believe, and smarter than you think you are."

In that moment I felt like this was a love note directly from my husband. These are the words he would have said if he was standing right there holding me in person. No doubt. He had often said, "You are so brave" to me, in the last year especially. Now I knew God allowed me to find this love note at this precise moment. When I needed it the most. Dave's words to me.

A few weeks later, my son's fiancée Heather said, "Do you realize where those words come from? They are from a Winnie the Pooh story." It turns out that it's an exchange between Christopher Robin and Pooh from a 1997 video.

Christopher Robin tells his friend, "If ever there is a tomorrow when we're not together...there is something you must always remember. You are braver than you believe, stronger than you seem, and smarter than you think. But the most important thing is, even if we're apart...I'll always be with you."

So the wall decal I found at the precise moment I was saying I just couldn't go on was actually sandwiched between some other meaningful words of comfort that were perfect for this very moment. "If there's ever a tomorrow we're not together" and "even if we're apart...I'll always be with you."

The thought that Dave bought that decal four years prior to my finding it was fascinating. Additionally, that he had never used it or even showed it to me was even more interesting, but most exciting of all was that those words were waiting for me as a precious, encouraging love note exactly when I needed it the most. What are the chances?

It doesn't surprise me that God allowed Dave's words to encourage me and give me some sort of comfort in this dark moment. Dave had lifted me up out of darkness quite a few times in our marriage with his love, care, and words.

Years ago during one of the most stressful and hardest seasons of my life, when I was hardly sleeping and walking through depression, I had gotten into the habit of saying, "I just feel overwhelmed" and "I'm so overwhelmed." Every time I'd say those words, I was unknowingly agreeing more and more with that feeling and I would cry and feel even more overwhelmed. Months went by like this—in a cycle of not sleeping, crying all the time, and saying I was overwhelmed by everything. He'd pray with me, hold me, and just listen. He was the most patient and kind human I've ever known.

I remember the day Dave looked at me and very seriously said, "Bear. Enough. I don't want you to say you're "overwhelmed" anymore!" It took me by surprise because he was never stern with me, but he was tired of seeing me in this state. He embraced me, prayed for me, and said, "Every time you say you are overwhelmed in a negative way, you are declaring that you are completely covered over and cannot breathe. You are agreeing with the feeling of hopelessness and despair. From now on you are not allowed to use that word any more unless you are going to say you are overwhelmed by the Holy Spirit. He's your Helper. You need to begin saying you are overwhelmed with peace, joy, and contentment."

Those words of wisdom coupled with the authority of a loving husband changed my life. It was a defining moment for me, and I began to use different words to describe how I felt but also began to speak the words I wanted to feel in faith over myself and my emotions. He would hold me and agree with me in prayer. Slowly and steadily I climbed out of the black hole I felt I was in. His words of wisdom were the rope I needed to grab on to and pull myself out.

Now, just a few days after the most traumatic and horrible day of my life, where I truly felt overwhelmed in the most negative way, he was encouraging me again with written words of wisdom he had left behind. He was reminding me I was braver, stronger, and smarter than I even believed myself to be.

My son David framed the treasure I found in the closet as a gift for me for Christmas. It is in a shadow box with little twinkling lights that shine behind the written words and is displayed in my bedroom. I often read and reread those words and imagine my husband smiling as he speaks them directly to me. He was my greatest encourager.

Dave knew and understood that my love language was words of affirmation. He also knew that the power of life and death are in the tongue. He was always careful about how he spoke to me. He chose his words wisely and if he was upset about something, he'd rather not speak than say something he'd regret. I always admired this about him.

Because Dave truly was a great husband who wanted to make me happy, he used his words carefully, intentionally speaking life into me. He would lift my spirit and my heart with his words; whether spoken or written in a card. Since the early days of dating, Dave gave me cards and love notes which I keep in a special box. All these treasured, handwritten words remind me, any time I wish to read them exactly how he felt about me and how much he cared. They are words of life to me.

One day, a few weeks after he went to heaven, I decided to go to the church to bring home some boxes with personal items. I began looking through boxes and came upon some things Dave had in his office. When I came upon a small Atlanta Falcons football, I completely lost it. I was glad I was alone because I began to weep and had a hard time pulling myself together. As I continued to look through other things with tears streaming down my face, I opened a book that I once had on my office shelf years ago. A devotional book for little girls called My Princess Devotions.

As I picked it up, still blinded by tears, I flipped it open to a random page. Not at all by coincidence, the heading read "No More Tears" with the following Scripture:

> *(God) will wipe away every tear from their eyes. There will be no more death or sadness. There will be no more crying or pain. Things are no longer the way they used to be.*

—Revelation 21:4 NIrV

God's Word, in His perfect timing aimed at exactly what I was experiencing at that moment! Words full of promise for a future without tears or pain. Amazing! That special God note was enough to fill my heart, but the tears continued to flow. I

picked up the next book in the pile and opened it only to the very front page behind the hardcover. There, surprisingly and unbeknownst to me, was a small card with my husband's handwriting! I was shocked! It read, "I pray blessings on your day today! And an unending joy! <3 u -Me."

My husband had apparently left this note for me in this book long ago for me to find on this very day when my heart was breaking with sadness over missing him. When he wrote that note, surely inspired by Holy Spirit, Dave merely thought he was leaving me a note of encouragement to be found as a surprise when I needed to see it. How right he was!

How marvelous is God that He would have all these things orchestrated for me to "stumble upon" in this perfect timing?

I'd like to say that these things brought me so much joy and comfort that I stopped crying, but I can't. I cried all the more! Tears of grief mingled with tears of gratitude for the goodness of my God and the great love of my husband. I felt embraced by my two greatest loves and their written words for me...in a very lonely place, surrounded by boxes full of memories in the church's storage room.

Judge Not

———— ⚬✢⚬ ————

Sometimes I just sit and stare. Numb. Just stare at nothing and everything. I don't know what I'm hoping to see. A vision of him? A dream while awake? A sign of some sort? I don't know. In those moments, I don't even know what I'm thinking. I'm numb yet in so much pain at the same time. It's so hard to explain. This hole in my heart. In the middle of my chest. I can feel it. It's a void; a gaping wound that can't be filled. I have been ripped in half. Yeah, that's how it feels, and sometimes, I don't know how to function. It's like for a moment I forget how to walk, talk, think. I'm just numb.

I try to remember. Remember everything. I don't want to forget anything. I struggle to remember every detail of every moment of our lives together because the fear of forgetting grips me and makes me anxious. Like I'm drowning.

Did I take all the moments together for granted? They were my "normal". I had such a wonderful normal. My day-to-day life was so full of perfect love that I had forgotten how it felt to not have it. Dave loved me so well. He never hesitated to serve me. He seemed to relish it, loved to make me smile. He never complained when doing something. He always went out of his way to do things for me, like stopping by Edgar's Bakery to pick up a slice of their delicious strawberry cake simply because he knew I loved it. We would sit on the couch in the evening, watching one of our shows on TV and share the slice of strawberry goodness. Most often, with just one fork. Back and forth we'd eat little pieces at a time and he'd always save the last bite for me. Always. He'd insist I have the last bite. That's true love.

When we'd go on trips long or short, he'd have the radio playing some sort of music you could sing along to. He knew every word to every song. It always amazed me because whether it was '80s rock, Broadway, Disney, contemporary, or worship, he knew the lyrics. Whatever came on the radio, Dave sang along. I would watch his mouth move and his head bob to the music and I'd smile and shake my head. My next words were always, "How do you know that song?" I always joked that he could go on one of those game shows where you have to finish the lyrics to random songs and win it all. He could have.

He could have also won it all on several other game shows. Who Wants to Be a Superhero?, Face Off, The Amazing Race, Steampunk'd, and pretty much anything else that involved design concepts, creating, costuming, makeup, or strategic thinking. The kids and I would often say, "You need to go on that! You'd win!" We meant it. I hoped it. The money he could win would be nice, but more importantly, everyone would get to see his talents and what he was truly capable of.

Of course, he was always a winner to us. We were his biggest fans. No matter what he did, it was impressive.

I really don't think he ever got to do everything he was capable of doing on this earth. He was the consummate frustrated and under-appreciated artist. I felt like he was not truly seen. Sure, people "appreciated" him and thought he was great, but he could do so much more than what others got to see. There was so much more in him and to him. David Smith was a genius, at least to me.

These are the kind of things I don't want to forget. They rush into my mind like a flash flood as I sit staring into the sky. Numb. Just numb.

The tears are always on the surface. Without warning, they come out. I'll be going about my day and see something that reminds me of him or someone says one word, just one word and here they come! One thought can immediately trigger the valve and whoosh, there they are, streams of tears that cannot and will not be contained. They can't be stopped. I just have to let them come. At times they show up in quiet streams, at other times they rush out accompanied by weird guttural sounds that surprise me, but are truly the deep expression of my soul.

I've cried over a lot of things in my life, but the weeping you do in grieving the loss of your other half is that of a dramatic movie scene that you've watched and always thought it was over the top. It seems that groaning and moaning while crying out your deep pain is a real thing. It's necessary. Now I know. You can't judge the way people express grief or what they do to deal with it. Especially deep pain like this, heart-wrenching pain. You can't judge it. You shouldn't judge it. Unless you've been there. Trust me.

I learned a hard lesson about judging grief on Sunday, November 19, 2017, just 5 days before Dave's passing. On Saturday, he told me that he'd like to go ahead and pack up his office. The church was moving to a new building in the coming months and the offices needed to be packed up and ready soon. Dave said, "I know I don't have to be packed up for another couple of weeks, but let's stay after services tomorrow and pack up my office before Thanksgiving, that way it's done and we don't have to worry about it."

Little did we know how important this would be for me and our kids.

His office was sort of a Captain America museum. That's what some jokingly called it, "The Museum". He had over two thousand pieces of Captain America collectibles displayed on shelves, walls, and any other spot that could be covered. When parents came into his office they were impressed. When kids came into his office, they were wowed and wanted to touch and play with everything they saw. Counseling or serious talks in that office were sometimes hard because of the massive display of red, white, and blue, or maybe in hindsight, they were actually disarming and comforting.

Behind his desk hung a huge piece of Captain America art he painted on two pieces of plywood. Side by side and overlapping just a bit, they made one big picture. My very favorite thing in that office was that particular mural because it was a work of his hands.

As planned, we stayed after church was over that afternoon. I ran out and picked up lunch at Carrabba's. We cleared off Dave's desk and had a picnic lunch right there next to the pencils and paperclips that needed to be packed. We took our time with lunch that day. Looking back I feel like the Lord wanted me to have that memory seared in my mind forever. We shared pieces of bread and that delicious herb olive oil stuff they give you. We talked, laughed and planned for the future. That was our normal, what we always did—talk, laugh and make plans. Always dreaming up something new. A new adventure we'd take. A new set he'd build. A new curriculum we'd write together. A new theme to collaborate on. New lessons to study and bring to life for the kids. Always inventing and planning.

This day we were planning what our children's ministry area in the new building would look like, what furniture we still needed to order, and all the construction work that was being done over there.

After lunch, we knew we'd have to get busy if we were going to get his stuff packed because there was so much of it! We cleaned up the leftovers and I started putting boxes together. Dave began to take down action figures, cars, motorcycles, and all kinds of random Captain America memorabilia off the black shelves that lined one wall.

With the empty boxes stacked and ready to receive the precious treasures, we began wrapping each piece in paper and bubble wrap. One by one he touched each one as if they all had special meaning to him. They did. He was intentional in giving them each special attention, sometimes stopping long enough to tell me what era it was from or in which movie Captain America wore that one uniform. I even remember asking him which was his favorite of all. He told me his top three.

Dave had only figured out a year or two before why Captain America collecting had become important to him. The memory came to him one day as he caught a whiff of Old Spice at the store. Like a flood, memories of playing action figures with his dad as a little boy came to mind.

He told me that his dad had bought him his first Captain America action figure as a child and said, "Son, this superhero is special because he loves his country, fights for justice and freedom, and stands up for what he believes in." From that moment on Captain America became his favorite.

Dave knew every piece in his collection. For birthdays and Christmas I'd have to double-check to make sure he didn't already have a particular one I'd found. Sometimes when people would want to get him a gift, they would text me a picture with "does he already have this?" I didn't know. I would ask him and he would quickly be able to tell me if he did or didn't already have it in his collection.

That Sunday we packed for several hours into the evening. Every one of the Captain America collectibles was in labeled boxes by the end of the day. I am so thankful now that he and I had that day together and that he was able to pack up his own stuff in the meticulous way he wanted to. I'm so glad I stayed to help and listened to him tell me all about his collection. We were making one more memory I can hold on to now.

At some point that afternoon, I stepped out to use the bathroom down the hall from Dave's office. I thought we were the only ones in the building, but that was not the case. I realized as I stepped out of the bathroom that there was some sort of meeting going on in the conference room across the hallway. The doors were open and I could hear the voice of a woman on a video that was being played on the big pull-down screen for a handful of people sitting around the big conference table.

I wondered what this group was. I thought it might be a Bible study or interest group of some sort. I stopped long enough to listen to a few words that told me it was a meeting for grieving spouses. This seemed to be a widows and widowers support group. On the way back out of the bathroom, I lingered for just a few seconds and heard the lady on the video say something to the effect of, "You'll be tempted to talk to your spouse first thing in the morning because that's what you're used to, but try to remember to talk to the Lord first." I rolled my eyes in judgement as one does when one has not walked in someone else's shoes and thought, "That's so weird! Who would talk to their dead spouse?"

I remember walking back in to Dave's office where he was busy packing. He asked me if I figured out who was in the conference room. I said, "Yes, apparently it's a meeting for widows and widowers. It sounds so boring, no wonder they're all sad. The video said something about not talking to your dead spouse before talking to Jesus. Who would do that? That's so weird."

Just five days later, that would be me.

Those judgmental words haunted me all too soon. It was just a day after Dave stepped into eternity when I found myself in his closet, clutching his shirts and groaning "Babe, I can't do this without you!" that I remembered the words spoken in ignorance just a few days before, "Who would talk to their dead spouse? That's weird." I began to cry harder at the thought of those careless words. Now I was the weird widow that someone else may not understand. I had to ask God to forgive me for my attitude and the words I had spoken when I did not know what in the world I was talking about.

You really don't know a thing until it's your own thing to walk out.

Personal experience is the only thing that truly teaches you.

Sadly, this one I wish I had never learned.

Signs in the Sky & The Man on the Moon

My husband loved anything having to do with planets, stars, and God's heavenly creations. He loved the Star Wars movies and Guardians of the Galaxy movies. Whenever he saw the Asgard scene in the Thor movie, he would say, "I feel that's what Heaven is like, but so much more! If humans are able to design something like that for a movie, imagine what Heaven really looks like!"

He loved flight and he loved speed. One of his greatest desires was to fly from one galaxy to another without limitations. He would say, "The first thing I'm going to do when I get to Heaven is challenge Jesus and the angels to a race from one end of the galaxy to the other." This personal desire was a reflection of the type of relationship Dave had with his Heavenly Father.

He was looking forward to eternal joy!

One year for Father's Day I gave Dave a flying machine (amphibious trike) ride experience in Chattanooga. He absolutely loved it. He was so excited to "fly." Like a kid in a candy store, the experience just wasn't long enough for him. He wanted to stay up in the sky.

The day after he went to Heaven there were several confirmations to each of my children that the Lord was going to give us signs in the heavens as to the extraordinary, eternal adventure Dave had just embarked upon. This would only be the beginning of the amazing, supernatural things that the Lord would allow us to experience. We began to experience very special moments that seemed intentional and orchestrated by the Creator Himself!

Just hours after Dave's passing, our home filled with friends and family. A family friend named David hugged my son David. He expressed his condolences by saying, "I'm so sorry, son." Immediately and without thinking, David responded, "Someone had to paint the sky." In that instant even he thought it odd that this was his response.

This same evening as Brittany was returning from having gone to Nashville to get her things, there was another beautiful reminder to look up. She had been distraught with grief, finding it almost impossible to deal with what had just happened hours before. Brittany decided to play her guitalele and sing worship to God as Seth drove her home. Through her tears, she found some consolation and comfort in the strumming of the chords and the words of a song by Rita Springer.

"Worth It All"

I don't understand Your ways
Oh but I will give You my song
Give You all of my praise
You hold on to all my pain
With it You are pulling me closer
And pulling me into Your ways

Now around every corner
And up every mountain
I'm not looking for crowns
Or the water from fountains
I'm desperate in seeking, frantic believing
That the sight of Your face
Is all that I need
I will say to You

It's gonna be worth it
It's gonna be worth it
It's gonna be worth it all
I believe this[1]

Brittany's thoughts were of Daddy. What was he doing right now? Was he doing exactly what he said he'd do when he got there? Was he flying and racing with Jesus across the sky?

Suddenly, her singing, playing, and prayers were interrupted by a phone call from her brother checking on her. As she answered the phone, she looked out the front windshield to see the brightest 'shooting star' she had ever seen literally cross the highway right in front of them! It took their breath away. Seth and Britt knew God was in that moment. To her, this was proof that Heaven is real because she was convinced God had let her see her dad flying just like he said he would.

As Brittany and Seth came through the door from having had this experience, they immediately began to tell us what had just happened. Their amazing experience brought us so much comfort. As they were speaking, Jonny, who had been in another room having a phone conversation, came out to tell us that Rachel's mom had just called and said, "Jonny needs to go outside and look at the sky."

We immediately decided that this was exactly what we needed to do. We all put on Dave's coats and hoodies, which although big on us all, seemed perfectly fitting in that moment. Stepping outside into the frigid November night, there was a flood of curiosity in our hearts as to what God was doing. It was so very cold, but the sky was clear and bright.

The seven of us went out to the driveway and stared up at the night sky. The black, velvety backdrop served up glittery, diamond-like stars that felt like they were shining only for us. We stood huddled together and shivering as shooting star after shooting star made a grand display in the sky above us. We all agreed that we had never seen anything like this! I had never seen so many shooting stars in my life, much less all in one night!

We couldn't help but think it might just be Dave up there flying at the speed of light with Jesus and his angels. We couldn't help but believe that God was allowing us to experience something unique and supernatural.

Each of us oohed and aahed as we caught glimpses of "our star" in flight. At times one or two of us would catch one that another had just missed. We filled the night air with, "Whoa, did you see that one?" as our laughter seemed to echo through the neighborhood and tears flowed down our cheeks. We all ended up lying on the ground in the driveway, shoulder to shoulder, watching the magnificent show in the sky with amazement. The greatest miracle moment came when Jonny said out loud, "Whoa, slow down Top Dog!" (his special nickname for Dad). Jonny then added, "You're going too fast! Slow down so we can all see you at the same time." We all got quiet and a few moments later, at the very same time, we all saw a wonderfully bright star begin its flight from our left to our right. It started out fast, then miraculously and literally, it hesitated in mid-flight for half a moment and continued on! We all gasped, then there was silence, then laughter...WOW! To my knowledge, meteors don't do that. That moment will forever be seared in our minds as a very special and supernatural gift from Heaven. The moment we saw Dad shoot across the sky.

*Three days later... **Man on the Moon***

It had only been five days since Dave had left for Heaven. Our family was still in deep shock and grief. We spent days together in the house talking, crying, looking at pictures, and reminiscing about the greatest man we've ever known. Our dear friends Nelson and Regina had just gone back to Texas that day. Seth returned to Nashville for work and Heather had to go home. Things had gotten quiet in the Smith household. I was in the bathroom getting ready for bed when I was startled by a great commotion in the house. I heard my son yelling, "Mom, come out here, quick! Dad is on the moon!" What in the world? Dad is on the moon? What does that even mean? I came out of my room to find David getting everyone to come to see what was happening outside. Quickly throwing on Dad's oversized coats and hoodies again, we all ran out to the driveway.

David then explained what happened. A few minutes earlier, he had walked Heather out to her car. She got behind the driver's seat and as he was saying goodbye, he glanced up at the moon that had, up until that moment, been hiding behind the clouds. As he did, he clearly saw his dad's face seemingly "sketched" on the surface of the moon. He was shocked and said to Heather, "My dad is on the moon," to which she replied a sort of "Bless your heart" sentiment, thinking he was clearly imagining things because of his grief. He said, "No, really.... look!" She stepped out of the car to look at the sky and there plain as could be, she realized David wasn't losing it... she could see it too! That's when

David ran inside to get the rest of the family to come to see this very strange miracle.

As Brittany, Rachel, Jonny, and I ran outside and looked where David was pointing, one by one we saw Dave's face on the moon! We realized this was something very extraordinary and it also felt like we had all lost our minds—but how can we all be crazy at the same time?

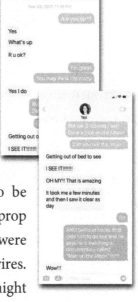

We marveled at the way the night sky looked that night. The clouds seemed to be hanging flat against the black sky, like prop pieces being held up by strings. They were moving back and forth as if suspended by wires. It was the strangest and most interesting night sky I had ever seen. The clouds would move gently side to side and hide the moon from our sight for a little bit, then part again and let us see what became a miracle to our eyes. I kept thinking, Am I dreaming or going crazy?

It occurred to me that maybe someone in another area or even state could possibly look up at the moon right where they were and see what we were seeing. I texted two friends and asked them to look up at the moon. Regina, who had been with us for several days, had just landed in Texas. She responded to my text that she would look as soon as she could get away from the blinding lights of the airport. Teri said she and Jeff would step outside and look. To our amazement, they both responded that they, along with their husbands, could see what we were seeing too, their friend's face on the moon.

Brittany called Seth, who had just returned to Nashville. She asked him to go outside and look up to see if he also saw what we were all seeing. He called a few minutes later to tell her that it was too cloudy to see the moon in Nashville. He was disappointed that he was not able to have the same experience we were having back in Madison. A few minutes later he sent Britt a text saying that when he went back in to his apartment, he was shocked to realize that the documentary he had been watching and had paused to go look at the moon was actually called Man on the Moon. This definitely served as a confirmation that we were not crazy. We could not have planned that!! But God did!

We stood outside in that driveway for over an hour and what we had been seeing on the moon didn't change, except to go from what appeared to be a "sketch" to a 3D relief image. The more we stared at it the clearer it seemed to get. It was truly amazing! We tried to take pictures with our phones and camera but could not capture what we were seeing. It was so very special and just for us.

The very next evening our neighbor stopped by to bring us a gift. All of a sudden he said, "Hey, did you guys see the creepy sky last night? I was coming home from work and I almost knocked and told you guys to come out and see it. I felt like you needed to see it. But I didn't knock because it was late." He had no idea that just a few minutes later we did, in fact, go out to see that amazing sky and the "Man on the Moon!"

In the days, weeks, and months to come we would continue to see amazing things in the sky. Every sunset was painted with colors that seemed brighter and more gorgeous than ever. Shooting stars welcomed our gaze. The clouds seemed to be sculpted like angels' wings. The heavens truly declare God's glory and the skies proclaim the work of God's hands!

To this day I step out into the night and stare at the sky hoping to catch a glimpse of my man on the moon.

The heavens declare the glory of God; the skies proclaim the work of his hands.
Day after day they pour forth speech; night after night they reveal knowledge.
They have no speech, they use no words; no sound is heard from them.
Yet their voice goes out into all the earth, their words to the ends of the world.

—*Psalm 19:1-4 NIV*

if i could,
then i would
jump up to the moon
and try to make some room

for someone else

if i could,
then i would
ride a shooting star
to wherever you are

to be with you.

Google Doodle Story

———◦⟨≫≪⟩◦———

It was a beautifully chilly evening in Nashville, March 20, 2018. Seth had prepared the scene to surprise Brittany. With twinkling lights, special photos, and their song playing in the background, Seth asked Britt to marry him. It was a beautiful evening celebrating love. Brittany's wish was that her dad could have been there. She questioned in her heart, was he watching from Heaven?

Lord, you know all my desires and deepest longings.
My tears are liquid words and you can read them all.

—*Psalm 38:9 TPT*

The very next day, we were amazed at God's love note! A friend texted me the following words: "I just turned on the computer and saw Pastor Dave in the Google logo this morning. Had to share it with you. Love you." I wondered what in the world she was talking about. As I enlarged the picture she sent of her computer screen, I was taken aback by the likeness! "Wait, that does look like Dave!" My friend's next text was, "He's in the stars!!" This friend did not know how significant this would be to us. She did not know that God had told us to "look at the sky" when Dave stepped into Heaven and this day's Google banner happened to look just like him...in the stars....

Not only was what seemed to be his likeness on this Google banner that morning, but all the added details were amazing to us. The face of the man in that logo looked more like my Dave at twenty-seven years old than the actual man they were honoring through the banner, (a Mexican astronomer). Interestingly, my friend did not know Dave at that age, but she said as soon as she saw it, she "saw him." The confirmation to Britt's wish to know that her dad had been watching from the heavens the night before was very creatively "drawn" in this banner. God has an amazing creative flair for communication!

Additionally, how very appropriate that this day was "World Puppet Day"! One of the many artistic abilities my husband had was designing, making, and bringing to life all kinds of unique & fantastic puppet characters. Dave was a master puppeteer and truly an "imagineer." I often joked that he had many personalities. If you ever got a chance to be present during one of our events or services, you definitely got to experience these crazy characters. Whether it was a sock with googly eyes or a one-of-a-kind, soft sculptured puppet, everyone watching would get lost in Dave's art and forget there was a human speaking for that piece of fabric and foam, myself included. I like to think that he's already had a chance to hang out and even create with Jim Henson & Walt Disney. I can't even imagine the wonderful art and fun they are creating without limits!

The face on the Google banner was at the center of the logo and most interestingly to me is that the name "Google" for the search engine actually comes from the word "googol" pronounced in the same way. The word googol means "equivalent to ten raised to the power of 100." That is 10 with 100 zeros behind it. In other words, an unfathomable number. That's who this man was to us…and that's what this picture literally expressed. My Dave, my children's father, now watching down from the stars was and is one in a googol!

GOD IS in the details and is ready to speak to you if you just open your ears, eyes, and heart. He is present. He loves you that much! I happen to believe with all my heart that Dave is getting to fly and enjoy the heavens, planets, and cosmos right now in a reality we couldn't even begin to understand in our wildest, limited imaginations. Why not? Our Father delights in giving us our hearts' desires.

In Psalm 37:4, King David tells us to delight ourselves in the Lord and He will give us the desires of our hearts. Most of us think that this refers to things on this earth. I believe it does but more so, I believe that our Father will take great delight and pleasure in welcoming us Home and surprising us with the greatest desires of our hearts. Even giving us personal tours of the galaxies He created.

According to NASA, there were some beautiful light shows God put on for us humans in the skies in 2018. One of them was actually on what would have been Dave's 51st birthday, January 4th. I'm kind of jealous that my sweetheart has a front-row seat to that spectacular light show, truly a Happily Ever After.

Those who are wise will shine like the brightness of the heavens, and those who lead many to righteousness, like the stars forever and ever.

—Daniel 12:3 NIV

Heaven's Shore

———— ❧ ————

I have been teaching and talking to kids about Heaven for over 25 years, yet I have learned so much more about Heaven since Dave's departure. From the moment he passed, Heaven came alive. I've never been more hungry for Heaven, and it's never been so close. It's never been more real. I like to say that it is because half of me is there now. It is also true that half of Heaven is here with me as well. It is now one of my most favorite subjects to talk about. I just can't get enough and continuously ask the Lord for more revelations of Heaven. It is my final destination and truest Home.

I suppose everyone has different ways they imagine Heaven. A lot of people who have not studied Scripture or have not thought about it any farther than a far off fictitious place found in a fairytale story may at the very least be curious. Religion without relationship makes the thought of Heaven a foggy destination to work for.

I have found that a lot of people have a hope that Heaven exists. They imagine an abstract concept of Heaven where they'll spend eternity sitting on clouds, playing a harp, smiling softly at fat baby angels in diapers. No wonder so many people think Heaven will be "boring". Oh, they have no clue!

Heaven is a real place. Another realm, a spiritual one, yet tangible and with an existence that pales in comparison to the one we know on this side. Heaven, God's Kingdom, is a place of utmost beauty and incomparable adventure. There are no human words that could be adequate to paint a picture of the wonders that glorious place holds.

Since Dave's heavenly flight, my kids and I have experienced many dreams, visions and revelations of what Heaven is like and what he is doing there. That may sound weird to some, but we can all find heavenly revelations throughout the Bible.

The Apostle Paul was almost stoned to death in Lystra (Acts 14:19). As a matter of fact, the Bible says that they "stoned him and dragged him outside of the city leaving him for dead". The next verse says that after the disciples gathered around him, he got up and went back into the city. Maybe they prayed for him and he was resurrected or healed. We don't really know what happened exactly. It's possible that Paul might have experienced what we refer to today as a 'near-death experience'. The point is that it is believed that he saw Heaven during that experience.

In 2 Corinthians 12, he talks about it. The words and terms he uses to describe what he saw are "visions and revelations." He says, that a "certain man" was "caught up to the third heaven." He adds that he is not sure whether it was "in the body or out of the body." When you read a little further you realize Paul is talking about himself. He tells us that he saw and experienced things that he cannot even talk about or put into words. These extraordinary things were so "out of this world" that he felt he would come off as boastful if he shared them! He felt he was not supposed to talk about them.

This same man who actually experienced the third Heaven, later tells us, "No eye has seen, no ear has heard, and no mind has imagined what God has prepared for those who love Him" (1 Corinthians 2:9 NLT). It's like he's saying, "You just wait! You're not even going to believe your eyes because on this earth, no one has even thought up everything God has waiting for you in Heaven!"

I have seen some beautiful places on this earth. I've seen gorgeous places in movies and pictures; some that have actually taken my breath away, yet this Scripture says "eye has not seen." I have heard soul-moving choirs, beautiful voices, and amazing musical orchestrations with the most wonderful instruments, yet this Scripture says "ear has not heard." In my limited imagination, I have dreamt of wondrous places. The people who are called "Imagineers" at Disney have truly come up with incredible rides, movies, pictures, creations…yet, this Scripture says, "neither has entered into the mind of man!"

So taking all this into consideration, we can gather that the Kingdom of Heaven could never possibly be described in human words. An earthly description would never do it justice.

Another disciple, John, saw Heaven too. He was actually commissioned to write about it. He did so in the book of Revelation. The things he describes there are sometimes hard to comprehend and are so fantastical that I think they could not ever be accurately depicted in the grandest of superhero or galactic movies.

The Bible does give us many references as to what Heaven will be like. One of my favorite verses is where Jesus himself tells us in the first verses of John 14 that in His Father's "House" (Heaven) there are many mansions. So there are houses, mansions, living spaces... why would there be unimaginably beautiful dwelling places if we weren't going to "live" IN them? I believe with all of my heart that He has designed and created these mansions uniquely to each of us. God is so into details! This can be seen by just looking at the design of all the different flowers and animals on earth. Why would He not be detailed in the design of my forever home? In the Kingdom that is so much bigger and elaborate than this earth we call home, with beauty without compare, I have a mansion designed by the Creator of the universe! You do too! Wow!

Treasure awaits us there! (Luke 12:33)

We will receive gifts, crowns and rewards there!
(2 Timothy 4:8, Matthew 5:12, James 1:12, 1 Peter 5:4)

These are just a few verses that tell us what God has for His beloved children who have been faithful to Him.

In John 14:3, Jesus says that He is going there to "prepare a place" for us. When I read this verse, the word prepare jumps out at me. When a special guest or someone you love is coming to your home for a stay, you prepare. What are some of the preparations? You clean the house, you decorate, you make sure their guest room is just right; light candles, maybe even put a mint or chocolate on their pillow. I'll go out and buy exactly what I think will make them comfortable and smile.

Another big part of preparations for a reunion or gathering with someone you're expecting is food! I like to make sure my guests have the food and drinks they like best. I make preparations. So, when Jesus says, "I am going there to PREPARE a place for you, that where I am you will be also," I get excited! Now I don't consider my primary gift to be hospitality, yet I know how to prepare a place for a guest. How much more a God who IS love?

God is the ultimate gift giver. I mean, He gave His own Son so that we could all join Him in His Kingdom…no bigger more expensive gift than His very own Son! So, what kinds of gifts is He preparing? What kinds of mansion designs has Jesus been preparing? I believe He delights in each and every one of His kids individually and uniquely knows each of our tastes, likes, and desires! Can you try to even wrap your brain around the things He has prepared for us?

What will Heaven feel like? First, to be with God who is love personified and to be surrounded by His perfect presence continually and eternally will be enough of a reward. To know ultimate contentment, safety and peace will be amazing. To be completely, utterly, and perfectly loved and accepted will feel like, well…Heaven!

No sin, no comparisons, no pain, no sickness, no shame, no lies, no betrayal, no misunderstandings; just peace, joy, and unity amongst its inhabitants. Living life in utter fulfillment, joy, and adventure. We will continually be creating, learning mysteries, traveling with friends and family, laughing, singing, dancing, playing, fellowshipping, resting and worshiping all to the glory of God because every detail of the life we will live there will be without blemish or darkness.

What about animals? Yes, there are animals in Heaven! We read in the Bible about the lion, the lamb, horses, eagles, and all kinds of other animals in Heaven. There are living creatures there, like and unlike what we've seen here on earth. I am convinced that there are species and designs of elaborate creatures small and great that we've never even thought of!

Will your pet be there? I believe so! Why? Because He cares about everything we care about. I believe our beloved cockapoo, Guinevere was waiting on Dave when he got there. I just know my mom's little poodle, Buddy ran straight into my dad's arms the day he crossed over. Several months after my father passed away, I had a dream about him. I saw him in Heaven. He looked young and so handsome! His hair was jet black and curly, and he looked to be around 30. He was kneeling in a garden with his hands in the richest brown soil I had ever seen. He looked up at me and gave me the biggest, most radiant smile. He nodded towards me and went back to planting. I knew in that moment that God had given me a glimpse of what he was doing. Working in his garden, just like he loved to do while he was here on earth. My Dad and little Buddy are having grand adventures now, but also making sure to take time to get the rose gardens ready for the day my mother gets there.

What does the landscape of this Heavenly world look like? For sure we know the Bible talks about streets made of translucent gold. If there are "streets" that means we are going places. Traveling to and fro. The Bible also says that Heaven is a country and a city. It also mentions the river of the waters of life, bright as crystal. Walls made of stacked, costly jewels of every color. Fruit on trees that give life. Celebrations, banquets, and all kinds of amazing things to do!

Angels, the redeemed, and all created things shining, living, and thriving without death, corruption, or decay. Being able to gather in the great throne room whenever we want to praise and worship the one and only true God in all His majesty and splendor. To see Him, the Creator of the universe with our own eyes in all His radiant glory, surrounded by shimmering rainbows of living color. Wow!

It was February 8, 2018. My son David and I were riding in the car together. He was on the hunt for the perfect engagement ring for his sweetheart and had invited me to come along. As we pulled out of the neighborhood, I turned on satellite radio. The volume wasn't up, but so very softly I recognized a familiar tune and voice. It was Bobby Darin singing a song Dave and I loved,

"Beyond the Sea." We had always related this song to cruising, which had become our favorite way to vacation, specifically because of the title line and the fact that they would often play it on the cruises we'd take. It's one of those oldies where the tune is very familiar; you've heard it a thousand times, but you really don't know the lyrics to the whole song.

As I turned up the volume on the radio, I said to David, "Oh, this was always one of mine and Dad's favorite songs because it would remind us of cruising." All of a sudden the lyrics came alive in that car and took on a brand new meaning. To be honest, in that moment, it was as if I was hearing the song for the first time ever. David and I looked at each other and he said, "I don't think I ever heard those words before." We sat in silence, intently listening to the lyrics. We both sensed this was a love note from Heaven. I teared up because if you switch only two words to have it be a female singing it… the words are so very meaningful….

Heaven's Shore

"Beyond the Sea"

Somewhere beyond the sea
Somewhere waiting for me
My lover stands on golden sands
And watches the ships that go sailing

Somewhere beyond the sea
He's there watching for me
If I could fly like birds on high
Then straight to his arms I'd go sailing

It's far beyond a star
It's near beyond the moon
I know beyond a doubt
My heart will lead me there soon

We'll meet beyond the shore
We'll kiss just like before
Happy we'll be beyond the sea
And never again I'll go sailing

I know beyond a doubt
My heart will lead me there soon
And we'll meet, I know we'll meet beyond the shore
We'll meet just as before

Happy we'll be beyond the sea
And never again I'll go sailing.[3]

This sweet experience in the car would have been deep enough, but there's more…and here is where the "What are the chances?" comes in.

One week later on the morning of February 15th, I remembered that I had not journaled about the experience. So I sat down first thing that morning and wrote out the lyrics to 'Beyond the Sea'. I wrote about the reasons we loved the song and what had happened in the car. I also noted how the ship reference was so meaningful because God had been speaking to me about ships and sailing through this storm and of course, the "it's far beyond a star, it's near beyond the moon" had me undone because of all the ways God had already been speaking to us through the stars, moon, and galaxies.

As I wrote, I closed my eyes and saw myself running into Heaven's shore one day, right into Dave's arms. We would greet like giddy little children, he'd embrace me tightly, grab my hand and say, "Come on, you have to meet HIM!" In my mind's eye, I saw us running together to Jesus, the three of us ending up in a huge hug, laughing and rejoicing together.

Then, in my journal I wrote the following words, *"One day I'll get to cross the sea beyond the stars and moon and run into his arms—he will run with me—hand in hand to our Jesus and I'll embrace HIM the One I owe my everything to and truly, life will begin—beyond the sea with our Heavenly Father, our Friend Jesus and Holy Spirit! I can't wait! The ultimate adventure you don't have to come back from!"*

The very next day I received a message from a friend... Kim wrote: "Just wanted to let you know that we are praying for you and think about you every time I hear this song. I remember listening to this album on the way to Pastor Dave's life celebration, hearing this song and knowing/telling Cayden that this was the way he embraced Heaven. We are so thankful for your faithful servant heart for our children. We love and honor you!"

I had never heard the song she was referencing until this moment.

It's called "Heaven's Shore"!

Wow! I was stunned as I listened to the lyrics for the first time...

The final rest on that day
When I lay my weary head on heaven's shore
The final breath is not the end
It's just the start of all that I've been living for
On that day when I am welcomed home

I will run like a child
To the arms of Your love
I will sing with tongues of angels
With those who've gone before
When I look upon Your face
The very moment I have craved
In Your presence forevermore
On Heaven's shore

To leave this place is to leave my fears
And step into the light of the glory of my King
I'll see in full and bow in awe
In the presence of my Savior's majesty
I can't wait, no, I can't wait

Singing hallelujah, I'll sing forever, I'll sing forever
Hallelujah, I'll sing forever
Hallelujah, when I reach heaven's shore[4]

I stood frozen because the lyrics of this song I had never heard before echoed what I had seen, felt and written the day before. What are the chances? This was God's confirmation once again that there is actually a beautiful golden shore in that Kingdom and one day, I will be reunited with my love and the One who is the greatest love of all.

One more thing happened...Just a couple of days later, I was getting ready for church. I had music playing on my phone. I was purposefully worshiping the Lord through the pain, memories, and emotions that church and Sundays brought now. I stepped into Dave's closet without thinking about anything other than "I just want to hug him." I embraced and kissed his shirts and wept. All I could think about was Dave's faithfulness Sunday after Sunday to Jesus, the children, and our church. I moved over and hugged his button down shirts with the embroidered compass and gear "Kids Quest" logo that he wore every Sunday.

Just outside the closet door, I could still hear the music playing in the bathroom. Random worship songs had been playing on shuffle, one after another on my phone. The song, "You Are Beautiful" by Phil Wickham began to play and I quietly begin to sing along in my heart as I cried and embraced the memory of my love who is so far away. I imagined him holding me, both of us swaying as we worshiped the Lord together. As I buried my face into his shirt and the tears began to flow again, the following lyrics rang through the air and pierced my heart:

When we arrive at eternity's shore,
where death is just a memory and tears are no more,
we'll enter in as the wedding bells ring
Your bride will come together and we'll sing,
Oh! You're beautiful! [5]

This would have only been a sweet moment of worship and the lyrics a perfect coincidence if not for the way He had already been revealing "Heaven's shore" to me in all the different ways the previous days. Not orchestrated. Not planned. Just God speaking through a third song to reveal His care, presence, comfort, and love.

It was truly a meaningful and supernatural God moment for me that I will hold on to until I am there, worshiping with Dave and all the redeemed at our Savior's feet. This was yet another reminder that God is near to the brokenhearted and that my sweetheart is on the other side of that beautiful shore planning adventures and waiting excitedly for the day I get to join him! We will run like children into Daddy's open arms!

Yes, God cares about our deepest sadness and our need to be reminded of His beauty and the beauty of eternal love that awaits us in Heaven.

Heaven is real.
My beloved is there now.
I look forward to joining him there one day.
I look forward to embracing my Jesus!

"There is a place called 'heaven' where the good here unfinished is completed; and where the stories unwritten, and the hopes unfulfilled, are continued. We may laugh together yet."

—J.R.R. Tolkien

Laying Our Child to Rest

A season of death and mourning was around the corner and I had no idea…God knew.

At one point, almost a year after Dave's passing, I had some time to scroll through the inboxes on my computer and clean them up a bit. I have a bad habit of keeping email after email for years. In the previous year they had accumulated to thousands. It turned out to be over 3 years' worth of old communications that needed to be trashed. Maybe this habit of not getting rid of anything comes from something I learned long ago in the days of working for a law firm in Fort Lauderdale, which was "document everything." This served as good advice, as I came to find out many times in the coming years when I needed proof, evidence, or confirmation of something that was said or promised. It has also been good to remind me of conversations or exchanges that I may have forgotten regarding so many different things.

This was the case on November 3, 2018, as I decided to go through and clean up my old emails. Email after email was easily trashed until I came upon a particular one that I had forgotten about. As I read the words in this email that I had sent to myself as a reminder a year before, I was stunned. Once again God reminded me that He is in every detail of our lives and knows how our story will unfold…from beginning to end.

Ten months before Dave passing I received a prophetic word of knowledge from a young lady.

**For those of you who may be reading this and don't know what a "prophetic word" or "word of knowledge" is, let me explain. I've said over and over again in this book that God is in the details and wants to speak to us if we are willing to listen. When we are living life with our hearts open to Him and expecting Him to speak, we will hear Him. Through the still, small voice of the Spirit of God, sometimes He will drop a thought, idea, "picture," or message into your heart and mind to let you know something special, a mystery that only He knows. It can be about the past, present, or future. Sometimes it will be just for you, sometimes it will be for a group of people and sometimes it's a personal message for a particular person. A "word of knowledge" refers to a message that can only come from the mind ("knowledge") of God and a "prophetic word" means that it is something that will happen in the future that only God knows about. These are gifts from God given to believers for the building up of others. There are many more spiritual gifts. You can find all of the "gifts of the Spirit" in the Bible in 1 Corinthians 12.

Back to my story…in January of 2017 Ashley, who had been a friend of my daughter's since high school, stopped me as we were walking out of the church building. She said, "I have to tell you something."

Although the first part of what she had to say seemed to make sense at the moment, the words that followed seemed very odd and strange. We were in the beginning process of a huge move. Our church was in the planning stages of moving into a new building at the time. We understood that the next season of our children's ministry, "Kids Quest," was about to be truly an unfolding of a promise and dream come true. For many years we had been waiting for the day that we'd move into a bigger building. God had shown us a "congregation of 500" many years ago. Dave and I had been dreaming, planning, and designing what the new Kids Quest areas would look like. We were in the beginning stages of talking to architects that would help align things to make the old high school library an awesome steampunk, time machine lab themed room where kids would learn about Jesus.

It was going to be a bigger and better, brand new, colorful, and exciting version of where we had been for the previous seventeen years. A place that the elementary-aged kids of our church would call their own. A place where they would be happy and proud to invite their friends. A safe place to learn about God's Word and grow together. A place overflowing with creativity where they could experience the presence of God.

We had been telling the kids for months of all the wonderful things we had planned for their new ministry areas as we encouraged them to bring in offerings for their building fund. Cleaning, purging, and packing many years of ministry at the old location was such a tedious job, but there was so much expectancy! There was great anticipation as we worked towards the goal of the "new building" and all that the future held there. There were moments where we were overwhelmed with the huge task that lay before us…so exhausted by the preparations, but still so excited for the season that was ahead.

That's where we found ourselves when Ashley stopped me in the new church parking lot and shared the following:

"I saw you in the middle of the new room at Butler, and spiritually around you, I could see a time-lapse of promise unfolding. In the vision I understood it as "giving birth" because it would be a process much like birth. Full of life and expectancy and anticipation, but coming in stages and taking time."

"Like any big life change, I saw you guys looking excited but overwhelmed with all that lay ahead. Yet every time you went to celebrate or rejoice, the burden of burial came over you. 'How can I be happy when I'm in mourning?' was the feeling I got. I also saw a vision of you in the process of burying something. This is a hard season for you. I saw a cold bitter breeze trying to blow over you guys, threatening your joy. But God is protecting it and you. In the midst of this season, praise Him still. Don't accept the verdict of death that circumstances are declaring. Do not believe the lies of death, but instead praise God. Nothing is dead until He has declared it so. Don't feel like joy can't come with mourning in the midst of the struggle. Don't prematurely bury, but instead let the Lord have the final say and God will turn your tears of sadness to tears of great joy. Don't let this bittersweet season make you bitter. The enemy is not the victor. I think this season is not so much about happiness, but about the abundant well of joy Christ is asking you to drink from so that you might have peace, for you and for your family. It is a sacrifice God is asking of you, but it is only because He knows it will be a warm blanket to you during this season and a testimony of victory to His glory in the next."

Wow! At that time, I had no earthly idea of what was to come in the next year. Not only would my husband abruptly leave for Heaven, but Kids Quest would evolve and change a little bit at a time until it didn't look like anything I recognized any more. Kids Quest as we knew it would also die with him.

I took on the "burden of burial" as Ashley's message said, not only for my husband but also for a ministry I carried, birthed, nurtured, fed, and watched "grow up" to a thriving 17-year-old. When Dave left, I wondered what my role in children's ministry would be. Who am I? What do I have to offer? Should I continue in children's ministry? We were a team and now it's just me.

I talked to God a lot about it. This had been a very important part of my life. I knew that I was not to take the helm of the Kids Quest ship. I was not ready, willing, or feeling like I would be the one to continue to lead it. Understandably, someone else would now take the leading role and pastor this congregation of little people. For reasons that I still don't understand however, He would not have me participate in all the changes that would come. I had to distance myself from my "child" with great pain and many tears, watching our dreams and plans for the future disintegrate into ashes.

Unfortunately, Kids Quest did not die suddenly and quickly like my husband mercifully got to go. I had to stand aside and watch it pass away. As if a pillow was being held to its face and the very breath of life was slowly snuffed out of it.

It hurt to watch it gasping for air. I would have much rather it would have all been completely changed and restructured all at once. Like ripping off the proverbial Band-Aid. It would have hurt terribly for a moment, but at least it would have been over with. Like a samurai of old, letting it end with a swoop of a sharp sword and allowing it to have an honorable death, rather than a long and agonizing disappearing trick.

I don't know that anyone knew or understood what I was going through as layers and layers of the things I loved so dearly were stripped from me. I was left with ashes. Not only me, but also my children. If this ministry was my "child", then it was their "sibling". My kids have also suffered deeply, watching it all die.

I endured many deaths in that first year. My best friend and ministry partner, husband, lover, and hero. Security, intimacy, happiness, plans, dreams…and a beloved children's ministry we had devoted our lives to…all gone.

Little did I know that Ashley's powerful words were a foreshadowing of events to come. The "burden of burial" would indeed visit me.

On the morning that the new children's ministry leaders were to be announced, I had a very meaningful and vivid dream. In the dream, I was driving a car to church. (In dreams, cars can often mean "ministry.") I parked the car in the back of our previous building and suddenly I realized I was no longer behind the wheel. I was now seated in the back seat behind what I could tell was a new driver at the wheel. I looked left, out of my window where I realized Dave had parked a car beside us. He had gotten out and was now standing by the open window smiling at me. He had a big bouquet of red roses surrounded by baby's breath, which he joyfully gave me through the open window. In the very middle of the center rose was a shiny black gemstone. I pondered the dream and realized it meant that although he was in "another car" now and I had spiritually been in the driver's seat after he left, it was now time to give the steering wheel to another. He was validating and celebrating my "retirement" from this chapter of life by giving me the red roses. Those symbolized love and passion, which we had served our ministry with. The baby's breath symbolized new life and a new beginning. The black gemstone symbolized death at the center of it all...and yet it all meant that beauty can be found even in death.

This dream didn't make complete sense until I pondered it during the worship service that morning. When I was asked to join the new children's ministry pastors on stage, surprisingly to me, but not by coincidence, I was given a bouquet of red roses surrounded by baby's breath, just like in my dream. God was confirming what I had seen in my early morning vision.

The letting go of this ministry was not easy and I don't think people understood how painful this process was for me and for my children. This was a huge chunk of our life; a huge investment of heart and soul.

That same day after the service was the last time I walked in to the old Butler High School library. Most everyone had left the building and the lights were off. I stepped into the large empty room which would have been a dream come true for us as the new Kids Quest. I went in slowly and sat quietly on the first row. I was having my own private funeral for this child of ours. Tears poured out of my eyes as I recalled all the wonderful lessons, times of worship, and fun we had been blessed to be a part of for seventeen years. I couldn't help but think of all the lives that God allowed us to impact through this part of our history. So many children we had the privilege of loving and praying with. So many teens we had the honor of mentoring in leadership. So many lessons written, themes planned, and stories told for the sake of the Kingdom of Heaven. So many great friendships were made. So many memories stored away in the crevices of my heart. I sat there on the front row of folding chairs in the dark for a long time thinking about all of this.

Then in a whisper that was louder than my pain, I heard God speak to my heart. "This isn't yours. You're done. This is just a legacy and a place of remembrance for you. That's all. You set the foundation. Walk away. Remember the flowers Dave gave you through the car window in your dream? They symbolized a gift towards your future; a gift of love and congratulations. The center of the rose was black which means death, grieving, and loss, but it was shiny like a precious stone because it's not to be viewed as a negative but as a God-given purposeful journey. Even in the deep pain that's at the center, there is beauty. It's surrounded by love and passion, which is symbolized by the red rose. Around that is baby's breath, which means a new beginning.

When a baby takes its first breath, it comes with a loud, excruciating cry for the start of that new beginning. Take the bouquet of roses, say thank you and walk away."

I did.

I have learned that Renaissance Belle is found both in birth and in death if we can manage to see through the tears.

Renaissance Belle, The Story

———————— ❦ ————————

August 3, 2017, will forever signify the start of the season of "new beginnings." We spent that day at the Magic Kingdom in Orlando where our son Jonathan proposed to his sweetheart Rachel at Beast's Castle.

The previous week Dave, Jonathan, Rachel, and I had been in Jacksonville, Florida, at New Life Church where we held a four-night family event called Pirates of Paradise Island. The theme, which included storytelling, pirates, puppets, and songs, was all about putting our trust in the ultimate Captain, Jesus, getting on board the ship, "Ecclesia", and sailing towards our ultimate destination, Paradise Island to be with Him forever.

It was a wonderful time and the very last family, week-long event Dave and I would do together. Looking back, I am so thankful we spent quality time with our Jacksonville side of the family as well. Dave got to enjoy time with his siblings, nieces, and nephews twice that year which was not the norm since we had lived out of the state of Florida for many years. In January of

2017 we had also taken a family vacation to Jacksonville because I felt in my heart Dave needed to celebrate his 50th birthday with his brother, John who was celebrating his 70th. Who knew that these two trips in one year, with all their treasured memories would be so meaningful and important?

God knew.

The marriage proposal had been in the works for several months. Jonny planned to pop the question in the park's Fantasyland, specifically where Beauty and the Beast meet and fall in love in the animated movie because it was Rachel's favorite. Weeks earlier, Dave and I put together a glass dome-covered rose like in the movie for Jonny to hide the engagement ring in. Miraculously and at the last minute, we were able to make reservations at the Be Our Guest Restaurant for breakfast and the plan was in motion. To Jonny's surprise, we flew in David and Brittany to join us at the park so that we could celebrate this very special day as a family.

The plan was that we would "plant" the glass-domed rose with the ring by the rose prop in the castle's west wing dining room just like Jonathan wanted. Everything went smoothly and at just the right time, Jonny walked Rachel over to the enchanted rose picture area where he reached for his own surprise. He knelt on one knee and asked his princess to be his bride. We spent the rest of this beautiful day as a family, laughing, playing, and enjoying each others' company. Finding favor at every turn. This perfect day ended with fireworks, hugs, and thankful tears for love and redemption.

The following day on our way home we decided to stop by a pet store "just to look." I kept telling Dave that we shouldn't get another dog. After all, only three years earlier we had to say goodbye to our sweet cockapoo, Guinevere. She had been a part of our family for almost fifteen years. It had been hard to let her go, but she had gotten so sick. We said then that we wouldn't get another pet so that we could be free to travel after the kids got married. In this new season of life, we didn't need something else to take care of. But Dave insisted that we would just look because, as he said, "I know puppies make you happy."

We looked at and played with many puppies, but as we were literally walking to leave the store, Jonny said, "Mom, look at that one!" There, with her nose pressed up to the glass was a tiny, black, sleepy-eyed creature that was the spitting image of our previous faithful friend, Guinevere! She was probably the only puppy we hadn't looked at in the last hour. This little one had been napping in a fluffy puppy pile facing away from the glass window the whole time and just as we were leaving, she woke up and turned to look at us. We couldn't get over our surprise. The pet store employee brought her out for us to hold and I knew it was pretty much over. I looked at her, looked at Dave, looked back at her and said, "No, we shouldn't." My husband's response was, "But you NEED her." Indeed! Little did we realize how much I would need her constant company and comfort in the months and years to come! We loved that her birthday was May 4th!

Unexpectedly, we ended up leaving the pet store with a brand-new 3-month-old pup! Another "new beginning." This cuddle bug rode perched on my shoulder like a little neck rest most of the way home. When we finally arrived at the house that evening, our son David challenged us to find a creative name for this new baby. After all, our previous pups had fancy names like Lancelot and Guinevere. This little one needed a little something more. After a lot of name searching and discussion, I went out to the back porch, sat, and prayed, "God, what is her name supposed to be?" The word "Renaissance" popped in my head. I had never heard of a dog named Renaissance. Since we already liked Belle, I went inside the house and asked my husband what he thought of "Renaissance Belle" as her name. We could call her Renni for short. Dave thought it was perfect, especially because Renaissance Belle meant "beautiful new beginning!" With so many new beginnings in our family and life, we knew it was a God-inspired name and a spiritual banner to be hung over our hearts.

Yes, we knew it...we felt it...this coming year would bring engagements and weddings, a new church building move with fresh vision for ministry, precious new babies in our extended family, entrepreneurial dreams would begin, and ideas would take shape for things we've had on our hearts for years.

We KNEW 2018 would be the year of "Renaissance Belle!" Beautiful new beginnings!

It would only be 3 months later that our family's life would suddenly come to a devastating crash as my amazing and beloved husband of 29 years stepped into eternity. The best husband and father ever. My Dave, my sweetheart, the love of my life. Father, son, brother, uncle, friend. Children's minister. Mentor, leader, writer & teacher. A hero and creative genius. Gone. *I was left wondering...what about our "Renaissance Belle," God? I thought 2018 would be our beautiful new beginning?*

I have wrestled with God about this. My Dave definitely got the ULTIMATE and eternal "Renaissance Belle" we all long for. He stepped into the Kingdom of Heaven in an instant. He ran into the arms of his Lord, Jesus. He ran to the embrace of the One he loved most. The One he had taught children about for 26 years. He most certainly heard, "Well done, my good and faithful servant." He is walking on streets of gold and flying throughout the galaxies like he dreamed about.

My children, although crushed in dealing with their great loss, would each begin a beautiful new chapter with the loves of their lives. These three amazing human beings found three other amazing human beings to love and be loved by to be their companions for the rest of their lives.

But, what about me? How was this supposed to be a Renaissance Belle for me?

One morning, I had a serious conversation with God. I was sad, upset, and quite frankly mad. Mad at the idea that Dave and I had planned on 2018 being a beautiful new beginning for us and now everything…everything…every single thing had changed for me.

I was now waking up each morning asking God, "Who am I? What now? Where do I belong?"

A request to model…

It was 1979 and I was 13. Let me paint the scene…It was the days of meeting up with friends at the roller skating rink and going around and around to disco music with your Farrah Fawcett-winged hair blowing in the breeze. Laverne & Shirley, The Love Boat, Charlie's Angels, and Eight is Enough were my shows. Teen discos were a thing and I was all about satin jackets, spandex, and colorful suspenders (like Mork wore on Mork and Mindy). One of my favorite things to do was make "slam books," and I had countless scrapbooks with all my favorite TV stars' pictures glued in them. My bedroom walls were covered in colorful posters of my star crushes, Shaun Cassidy, Leif Garrett, and Donny Osmond, which I had cut out of my Teen Beat magazines. (I just knew if Shaun had the opportunity to meet me he would fall madly in love and we'd get married.) Like most young girls, I wished to be a star.

I would stare at pictures of who I thought was the prettiest star at the time, Jaclyn Smith, and wished I was her. If we ever played Charlie's Angels with my friends, I HAD to be Jaclyn, I mean I had the long, dark hair and my name was Jacqueline, so—duh. Yes, we spelled it differently and my last name was Rodriguez, quite the opposite of Smith, but I hoped one day to "be" Jaclyn Smith. I even practiced signing my name over and over. Little did I know I would grow up to marry a Smith and literally be Jacqueline Smith! God has a sense of humor and knows even the most trivial desires of our hearts.

When an announcement was made at school that the Fort Lauderdale Barbizon School of Modeling was looking for new stars, I just knew this was destiny knocking. I begged my parents to take me just to see what it was like and I dreamed that maybe, just maybe, I would be "discovered." I mean, their advertising promised, "Be a model. (or just look like one)." Literally, that's what the ad said. Maybe I could be a model or at least look like one? I don't know how I talked my mom into taking me to the storefront location on Commercial Boulevard, but she did. After a lengthy informational talk to a group of about 50 girls and their bored parents, we pretty much all got the classic, "Sure! We can work with your daughter, she has great potential. Here's what we charge." After hearing what the fee was, we got up and left. In a matter of hours my dream of being a runway supermodel ("or just looking like one") came to a screeching halt. There was no way my parents could or would afford whatever the expensive price was at the time to make their kid a star. I'm sure I was disappointed, but to be honest, I went on into teenhood and completely forgot about being the next Cheryl Tiegs. I laugh now thinking about how silly it all was.

Fast forward forty years…

It had only been three months since Dave's passing, and I was having a hard time getting out of bed one particular morning. I had errands to run and it took all the strength I could muster just to think about rolling out of bed and out from under the grey grief cloud that surrounded me. I just lay there in my very empty bed, thinking about my great loss, staring at the ceiling, tears rolling down my face. Hundreds of thoughts swirled through my mind like scattered leaves in an autumn windstorm.

"God, I'm going to need you to help me walk today. I don't think I'm strong enough to hold my life and thoughts together, much less my broken heart. How do I put one foot in front of the other? How will I function now? Dave and I were truly one, and now I feel like half of me is gone. I have been ripped in half. I don't know how to walk with only one leg. You're going to have to help me figure out how to walk."

Immediately I heard Him speak to my heart, "I want you to model." I questioned him, "What?! What do you mean? How in the world do you want me to model when I can't even stand, much less walk." Not moved by my endless questioning He continued, "Like a model on a runway."

"But God, models, especially those on runways, are graceful! I am not feeling very graceful." Unfazed, He continued, "You will model grace. You will be full of grace. You will be covered in MY grace and model it for others to see."

"Lord, I've never seen a one legged model. I will probably stumble and fall on my face."

"I will teach you to walk again. It won't be like before. It will be different. It will look different. You will walk differently. I will give you a prosthetic."

That was a weird thing to hear. A prosthetic leg is an artificial limb. Not the real deal. My husband was the real deal. When we were married, we truly became one. We morphed into this beautiful, supernatural state of walking together, living together, loving each other and functioning as one. Now he's not here. I felt lost. I felt like I just couldn't walk without him. Seriously, stuck and unable to function. But I needed to walk. I needed to function. I had to keep on living. There's no other option for me. I must continue on this road.

Yet, this journey is now completely different. The trauma I have suffered from his death is palpable. I am not the same person. I am a changed woman. Emotionally changed forever.

I am half.

I understand that not all women completely feel this way. I have heard some say, "I am already whole and he doesn't complete me." That's fine, but that's not my experience. Yes, I was already "complete" but the way our story went, when Dave came into my life and we committed to a forever love and marriage, he somehow morphed within me in a swirl of completeness I would have never had otherwise. Another level. He complemented my existence. This is the kind of love we had. We loved being one. One in love, thoughts, decisions, home life, care for our kids and ministry. We just were. So, now without him, I feel…half.

God continued the conversation by saying, "Yes, I will give you a prosthetic and I will teach you to walk again. It won't be the same. It will feel weird and strange, but you WILL walk. Slowly at first. You'll have to get used to this new walk. You will walk differently. Your gait will be different. You will walk with a limp at times, but the more you walk, the easier it will become. Every once in a while you will limp and people will detect something is not quite right, but this will be simply for them to ask what's happened. You will be able to share your story, your journey and how you've learned to walk again. You will tell them and you will model grace."

"But God, models are graceful. I am not graceful right now. Far from it! I cannot be graceful if I'm limping and walking funny with a prosthetic leg." He continued, "You will model my grace, it's what will carry you. You may not "feel" graceful but those are the moments you'll be full of grace. My grace is sufficient."

Then He asked a question, "What does a runway model do?"

"They model the season's fashion."

"Yes, you're right. The model's job is to walk and show off the designer's garments for others to see, admire, desire and purchase for themselves. The model's purpose is to highlight the creator of the fashion they are wearing." Immediate revelation as to what He was saying dropped in my spirit, although I did not want to hear it in that moment. He ignored my mind's protests. I am no longer a silly 13-year-old girl dreaming of being a model.

This time, as a grown up, I wasn't looking to model anything. I didn't want to now. This time I was not a willing participant. This time the cost was a lot higher and one I didn't want to pay. My reluctant argument with Him continued.

God said, "You will wear grace. You will walk and show off my design. People will see and want what you're wearing for themselves. They will want the Creator's garments. You are now wearing my winter collection, called Renaissance Belle, beautiful new beginning."

"Wait, Lord. How is this new beginning beautiful? It doesn't make sense."

"Didn't I say I would give beauty for ashes?" As I heard these words, immediately my mind went to the box which sits on my dresser which literally contains my beloved's ashes.

"God, I know you have said beauty for ashes in your Word."

I searched for the verses in Scripture. I had read this passage many times before, but now they seemed to jump out at me in new revelation. "… to give them a crown of beauty for ashes, the oil of joy for mourning, and a garment of praise for the spirit of despair. So they will be called oaks of righteousness, the planting of the Lord, that He might be glorified" (Isaiah 61:3 Berean Study Bible).

Renaissance Belle means beautiful new beginning. A beautiful new birth. It was a promise from God and somehow in the face of tragedy, a promise kept by God, because He doesn't lie. Because He is faithful. Because He has proven to be true.

I have chosen to believe there is a
Renaissance Belle in my new season.
I have a great hope of finding beauty
in this new beginning,
even if it means digging through
the ashes to find it.

"For I know the plans I have for you," declares the Lord,
"plans to prosper you and not to harm you, plans to give
you hope and a future."

—*Jeremiah 29:11 NIV*

Cap's Girl

As much as Dave was Captain America, I was his Wonder Woman. He called me by this nickname often since the day we were married. It's funny because I loved the Wonder Woman TV show when I was little with Lynda Carter in the lead role. As a 3rd grader, I always got to be Wonder Woman when we played superheroes in school at recess because I had black hair and I was taller than the boys. I remember trying to imitate her stance and would actually grab the boys who played "the bad guys" by the arms to swing them around in circles. I would let them go at just the right moment, flinging them far away dramatically. Saving the world from obvious danger! You're welcome!

Dave began giving me Wonder Woman collectibles a long time ago and my office slowly began accumulating the Amazonian superhero dolls, mugs, and books. It always made me smile that he would think of me as "his" Wonder Woman. This turned out to be something that people associated with "us" and lasted throughout our 29 years of marriage. For many years in our children's church, Kids Quest, the leaders in the sound booth would play the Wonder Woman theme when I stepped on stage to greet the kids. We were always Captain America and Wonder Woman; in love with the red, white, and blue and each other. Although the comic book heroes are from different universes, we did a good job uniting them in ours.

Dave's Captain America collection was in full display in his office. It was quite extensive and impressive, making it an interesting stop for anyone visiting the church building, especially kids. It was normal for guests to be taken by the classic comic book enthusiast's mini museum for a fun side trip. Like the kind of random exit you take off the highway to see a special curiosity on your way to grandma's house. You're not sure what it's all about, but you're so glad you did it.

Dave often told me that when he passed away he wanted a party. He would say, "I won't be there, so don't have me in a coffin for people to look at. I'll be having a party, so you better have one too. I want upbeat worship, balloons, a full-blown party!" So, for his life celebration (we refused to call it a funeral) three days after he passed away, everything was decorated in red, white, and blue as a nod to his favorite superhero and in honor of our very own hero.

Family and some of our ministry leaders set up a walk-through line that took people through Kids Quest, which was decorated with dozens of Dave's creations. Set pieces, props, costumes, drawings, puppets, and other creations that had been used throughout our ministry were on display for people to remember and admire. I was overwhelmed with love at the attention to detail and care that had been given to display Dave's handiwork. He would have approved.

A friend made a special logo with Captain America that said, "In Honor of Dave Smith" that was put on t-shirts. Pictures of red, white, and blue Cap shields were all over social media 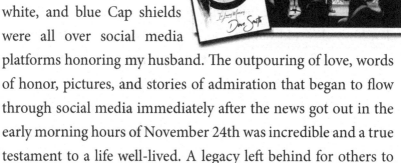 platforms honoring my husband. The outpouring of love, words of honor, pictures, and stories of admiration that began to flow through social media immediately after the news got out in the early morning hours of November 24th was incredible and a true testament to a life well-lived. A legacy left behind for others to imitate and follow.

For the celebration, everyone was encouraged to wear Captain America tees and we later heard that Huntsville and the surrounding cities were sold out in a matter of days! I was told that people had actually driven out of town to find Captain America t-shirts to wear. We were absolutely shocked and amazed at the way people turned out in the middle of the day on a Monday to honor and pay respects to my wonderful husband.

My children and I stood for hours greeting family, friends and even some strangers that came through to give us a hug. Most people just shook their heads and cried not knowing what to say. What could you say? There were no words people could find to express how they felt. We were all in utter shock and unbelief that this strong, healthy man, clearly loved by so many, was suddenly gone. Through my fog of grief, I kept telling people that I released them from having to use words. There were no words and everyone felt it.

I was devastated and could hardly think straight. It felt like I was in a dense cloud I'd never be able to get out of. Despite wanting to fall to the floor in pieces, I was determined to stand. For him…I would stand to honor my hero. I refused to sit while what seemed to be a thousand people came through the line to greet us. I remember that some dear friends stood with me on that day. They literally had my back. Precious people and families stood in line for hours out the doors and down the sidewalk. The service ended up starting late because of the crowds that showed up that day. They had to cut the reception line short at one point to get the life celebration started. It was the most beautiful tribute

I had ever been to or seen for a hero's departure from this earth.

It was truly a heavenly party that unfolded that day with so much love to honor David William Smith. Having my children, family, and closest friends sitting beside me gave me so much comfort. Surprisingly, I felt strength I never knew I would be able to have in a moment like that. The strength that can only come from a supernatural place along with the peace that passes understanding.

One of our nephews put together the program for the celebration, a tribute in and of itself. Covered with pictures of "us" and of course, Captain America. The inside cover read as follows: *"Doesn't matter what the press says. Doesn't matter what the politicians or the mobs say. Doesn't matter if the whole country decides that something wrong is right. This nation was founded on one principle above all else; the requirement that we stand up for what we believe in. No matter the odds or the consequences, when the mob and the press and the whole world tells you to move, your job is to plant yourself like a tree beside the river of truth and tell the whole world... no, you move."* ~ Captain America[6]

This was my man. Steadfast and faithful, planted in truth. His demeanor carried stability for me, our kids, and even for the rest of the family. Like one of the nieces said, "When we were all gathered in a family setting, he sometimes didn't say much, but there was peace in our midst." And that was a feat because my side of the family is Spanish and loud!

Yes, he was my steady hero.

Captain America "love notes" are not uncommon. One

happened when Brittany had bought a couch on Craigslist a couple of months after Dave's passing. She and Seth went to pick it up from the seller. It was the last thing in his apartment because he was getting ready to move. When Seth and the man carried the sofa out and put it up on the back of the truck something fell out and rolled. The men didn't even notice, but Brittany was stunned to see a small Captain America shield right at her feet. The owner of the couch said he had never seen it before.

It was two days before my birthday in March and I just knew that somehow I would get a love note that was to be my birthday present from Dave. I had gone in the garage that evening searching for something random, but I ended up in a daze, standing in front of his workspace, looking at Dave's creations and bawling my eyes out. I finally sat in a folding chair looking up at the soft-sculpted puppets he made long ago and which had almost become like family members—Blu, Ping, Star Man, Comet Boy, and the rest of the characters that brought so much joy, laughter, and the Word of God to thousands of children and adults. I thought about how he had not only thought up those puppets on the shelf but designed, made, and created personalities and voices for each of them. He could do two at a time, talking to each other and to me on stage and not get their voices or personalities mixed up. I was always amazed by that.

Thinking about him and all the wonderful things he had made and brought to life, I sighed deep and hard, wiping away my tears. I whispered a thought out loud, "I was sure I'd get a love note today, God and I haven't, but the day's not over." No sooner had those words come out of my mouth, I glanced over to my left and for no particular reason, just began to move some boxes around that were stacked one on top of another. The bottom box was a hard plastic file folder box with a handle. I'm sure I had seen it over the years, but never really paid attention to its contents. I said out loud, "What's in there?" I opened the box and found treasure!

"My tears led me to treasure!" was all I could say. This box contained artwork dating back to our first years of marriage when he was doing t-shirt designs for Fort Lauderdale Beach souvenir shops. I grabbed the box and quickly brought it in and set it on the kitchen island. It was just me, my tears, and this long lost treasure box. I thought to myself, "It's my birthday present!"

Opening the box, I was flooded with memories as I began to take one manila folder out at a time. There were at least 50 folders filled with sketches, logo designs, magazines his artwork was featured in, newspaper clippings from when he won the sand sculpting contest on Fort Lauderdale Beach, and many other drawings. I began taking pictures one after another and sending them to the kids through texts. They responded with "Keep them coming!" Looking through this box and dozens of folders filled my heart with joy and made him feel so close. Memories began to pour into my mind. *So thankful I have this*, I thought.

About two hours later, after poring over each and every piece of artwork in the box, I sighed and said, "Thank you, God." At that moment I noticed that there were about four more manila folders at the very back of the box. I figured these were empty. They looked empty. They were… except one. One last folder had only one drawing in it. I pulled it out and to my surprise, it was a drawing of Captain America and Wonder Woman in a passionate embrace and sharing a kiss! I had never seen this drawing before. I was taken aback by the clear representation that this artwork was of "us!" Ah! THIS was my birthday gift! Of course, I cried, I laughed, and I thanked God for my beautiful, intimate, and perfect love note.

How amazing is it that it is signed and dated 2004 and I had never seen it… until I needed it the most. It is now my favorite birthday gift of all time. Thank you, darling for drawing "us" as cartoon heroes! Your Wonder Woman loves you all the way through to eternity.

I will forever be

"Cap's Girl".

"When you believe beyond what your eyes can see, signs from Heaven show up to remind you love never dies."
~ Author unknown

Say Yes To Adventure

In a page from my journal entry dated April 2, 2017, seven months before Dave passed away, I wrote: *"In the story of our life, the end of one chapter means the beginning of another. Sometimes it's painful turning the page... but you won't know what's next unless you look. You won't know the adventure ahead unless you're brave enough to turn that page. In my story, you will find joy and pain, victories and failures, fear and faith, passion, and promise... and it's not over. There's more. I will be brave and turn the page because I don't want to miss anything. Even the scary parts will teach me and hope will carry me. #lifestory"*

Looking back now, I feel like those words I wrote were prophetically inspired to encourage and help me now. Little did I know that the chapters ahead were scarier and sadder than anything I could ever have imagined. I promised myself to be brave and turn the page...

I have reluctantly accepted that God wants me to "adventure." He has said for me to say "yes" to adventure and new things. This is so hard for me. I never wanted to or would have imagined having adventures without my best friend. This message of "adventure" had been burning in my heart. I couldn't ignore it. Say yes to adventure? What does that even look like? What adventures am I supposed to be going on or looking for, God?

It was Sunday, June 11th. Throughout the morning I had been thinking a lot about what God had been saying. After church that day, I texted several people to see if they wanted to have lunch. It seemed everyone had other plans. Sundays are hard as it is, but walking out all by myself feels awful. For so many years there was always a plan for after church lunch… now I just walk out by myself feeling like something is missing.

I headed home thinking about what I might want to eat. I decided I would go through a drive-through and take it home. I pulled into Zaxby's, but at the last second, I decided on Panda Express, which is right next door. I never eat there, but for some reason, I just pulled into the drive-through and ordered.

When I got home, I found one fortune cookie at the bottom of the bag. Still pondering what God had been speaking to me  about "adventure," I cracked open the little shell and read the note inside, "New challenges and adventures await." I felt in that moment that God confirmed to me in this most tiny note what He had already been speaking to my heart.

God speaks. Always. You just have to be willing to hear Him. Normally adventures, journeys, and trips are planned. You look at all your options. Where you'll go, where you'll stay, what you'll see, what you'll eat, and how much your budget is. You even pack accordingly. But this "grief trip" I am on was not planned. This journey I have been set on, I did not see coming. There was no way to even pack accordingly.

Dave was all about "experience" and "adventure". He loved a good adventure story. Whether it was Star Wars, Captain America, The Never Ending Story, The Wizard of Oz... westerns, mysteries, superheroes, whatever. Anything that had an outlandish adventure story was his favorite. The more saber swings, galactic blasts, and speeding flying things the better.

Something that many people did not know was that Dave loved horseback riding and longed to ride "wild and free" without restrictions. He often told me about a friend he had when he was in high school whose family owned several horses. They invited him to ride on the beach once as a teen. He was able to ride fast & furious along the Florida shoreline and absolutely loved it. Ever since then, he looked for opportunities where he could ride again.

He didn't get to ride very often, but every once in a while when we'd visit places with horseback riding adventures, he'd always jump at the chance to do it. Unfortunately, every place we ever went to ride was one of those ranches where you have a guide and everyone rides in a line behind him and his horse slowly along a trail. Dave's question to the guide was always the same, "Can I take him out and break free?" He'd always get the same answer, "No sir, you have to stay with the group." He'd ask the question every time knowing full well the answer would be "No," yet he asked anyway... just in case. Looking back now, I wish we had found a place where he could have done just what he wanted.

Early one morning not long after he went to Heaven, as I was in that in-between stage of sleep and awake, I heard, "Palomino. Dave has a palomino." As I began to wake, I was saying those words out loud in agreement with what I was hearing, "Yes, Dave has a palomino." I opened my eyes, now fully awake, and said, "Palomino? What's a palomino?" I knew it had something to do with a horse, but that was all I had an understanding of. Immediatley, I Googled "What's a palomino?" There, I found out that "palomino" references the color of a horse with a gold coat. A golden-colored horse! Of course he has a

palomino! Immediately I was reminded of Dave's great desire to ride. In that moment, I knew beyond a shadow of a doubt that God had a beautiful golden palomino in His Kingdom waiting for Dave to ride "wild and free" as he had always wanted. I wonder what he named him?

There were so many things Dave wanted to do and experience that, regretfully because of my own fears, I didn't "let him." I would say, "No, I don't want you to die". He'd say, "But it's fun!" He often joked that when he turned 70 and just "didn't care what anyone thought anymore" he'd go skydiving, naked! It was a joke...I think.

I should have let him skydive. I should have let him get that motorcycle he wanted. I should have let him bungee jump. I should have made a way for him to scuba dive. We should have hopped on a hot air balloon ride. We should have gone horseback riding more than just on a trail. Should have...those are words that cannot be fixed. You can't go backward and change the past, no matter how bad you want to.

One of my greatest regrets is not being brave enough to adventure more with him. Not the skydiving kind, I don't regret that extreme kind of fun. But, I should have said yes to more adventures.

Most of our marriage, I sat out on riding the tallest, loopiest, and fastest roller coasters because of fear. I encouraged him to ride with the kids and I'd sit and watch them from the ground. I know it would have made him happy to have me ride with him. Fear often kept me from experiencing more wild laughter, uninhibited screams, and joyful abandon with my best friend.

Here's something I've learned...don't let fear keep you from adventure; don't let fear keep you from making memories. Fear will paralyze you if you let it.

Practicality also kept me from adventure. Most adventures Dave longed for were expensive, so my practicality would say, "We can't afford to do that" or "We can't waste money on that." What I didn't realize was that what I couldn't afford was to waste time with worry, fear, and reservations.

Looking back, I now see that on so many occasions where my husband longed to leap from heights and fly free, my "practicality" and fear kept us grounded… literally. In the latter years, however, I did become more and more brave… he taught me a little at a time to "let go and enjoy the ride" and as long as he sat next to me and held my hand, I would be okay. Well, it was more like me digging my nails in his arm and screaming, but still—I rode more roller coasters in the last few years than I ever had in my whole life. With him by my side, those scary moments were not so scary. Even if they were, I felt safe near him. He was always my safety net. Whether riding the tallest roller coasters or riding all my emotional roller coaster years during a deep time of depression. He was there, holding my hand, riding with me. He never let me ride alone. He never let go of my hand.

Now this roller coaster of grief and mourning has me scared to death, sick to my stomach, and wondering how I got on it without my own permission. He's not physically here to hold me, speak words of comfort to me, or tell me I'm brave, but it's almost like I can hear him say, "Bear, you got this. You're not alone. The Lord has you. God's going to see you through. I'm so proud of you."

Since Dave's departure, God has told me, "You must say yes to adventure!" I have a desire to try new things in Dave's honor. I believe with all my heart he gets to watch, and I know he's proud of me for even thinking about doing something crazy or out of my comfort zone. I know he laughs with joy when I accomplish something new. I have decided to do things that may be uncomfortable simply because he'd love it.

I had the opportunity to visit a lifelong friend in St. Augustine May of 2018. I mentioned to Silvia over the phone while planning my visit, that God had told me to not let fear keep me from adventure. Being the kind of friend she is, she arranged for Brittany and me to go zip lining. Zip lining in and of itself is adventurous enough for this girl, but this particular one involved climbing up wooden ladders onto high platforms and walking across suspended rope bridges onto more platforms up in the trees. For those of you who don't mind heights, this may not be a big deal, but for me, it was quite the challenge!

The thought of zipping through the air was intriguing, but I wasn't too thrilled about being up high in the sky. Of course, how else are you going to zip down a line if not from up high? Maybe I was hoping for a special one just for me, maybe only 6 feet from the ground.

I had done this only once before at the encouragement of my adventurous husband, but I felt secure simply because he was near, cheering me on. This time, he wasn't physically with me to cheer me on, but I asked God to open up a window in Heaven and let him watch his girl conquering her fear of heights.

I decided I was going to do it, over and over again inside my head. I kept telling myself, "You can do this" all the way there. Sometimes to accomplish a frightening goal, you may just have to do it scared and all. I resolved to do it mostly to make Dave proud. I also did it because I thought it was important to face this fear. Additionally, I didn't want my daughter to think I was a big baby and I definitely didn't want to hear it from Silvia. In my mind and heart, I thought, *This will be one of the first of many adventures to come without him, but for him.*

Brittany and I arrived at the location, where they proceeded to have us sign releases and harness us up. Any time you have to sign a release, well that might just be a sign that you're about to undertake an adventure. Once we were in the harnesses, I knew there was no turning back. Technically, I could have actually turned back, but I was determined to do this. I began to feel like the Lord was going to use this experience to speak to me concerning the journey I was on, so I determined to continue on with my spiritual eyes and ears open to the voice of the Lord.

My first challenge was to climb a wooden ladder to the first platform. I didn't think I had the physical strength to do it. I was a little embarrassed at the thought that I may actually not be able to perform this first task. I had to push hard to get myself up that ladder. I had to follow through. This "experience" had already been paid for, it was set before me and I had to stick to my commitment to finish… and finish well.

That was spiritual lesson number one: Your life story has been written and paid for, so face forward, one step at a time, determine to finish, and finish well.

A few months after Dave's passing, Jonny and Rachel gave me a wall plaque that said, "You never know how strong you are until being strong is the only choice you have." It was so applicable to the life journey I was set on and also now, quite literally in this moment. With this first challenge, I would have to put that into practice. I was determined. Committed. I was doing this. I tried to look fierce, externally anyway… as "fierce" as a 5'2" lady in a harness and helmet could look. I took one step up

at a time, one hand, the other, one foot, then the other. I grabbed on to rung after rung with tenacity thinking the whole time, "I can do this. I have to do this." My hands hurt. My legs hurt. My pride was

beginning to hurt. "What if I really can't do this first, silly thing?" I climbed all the way to the platform. I don't know how many rungs were on that wooden ladder, but to this 52-year-old woman, they felt like a thousand.

Finally at the top, and celebrated by my daughter and the

instructors, I felt accomplished. You would have thought I had climbed Kilimanjaro, but it was just the beginning. I scooted quickly to the center of the platform and grabbed on to the huge pole in the middle, shaking on the inside and outside. (I'm sure the climbers over in Tanzania did not do this!) The guide asked, "Are you ok?" and before I could answer, my daughter said, "You did it! I'm so proud of you!" It was the encouragement and motivation that I needed to face the challenges that were still before me. Crazy how just a couple of sincere words from someone you love and you know loves you can spur you on.

That was lesson number two: When undertaking a challenging journey, bring along encouragers.

All of a sudden, I realized that this was only the beginning. Now I had to look to the next step... actually zipping off the platform. Wait, what? Oh yeah, the zip lining part...

"Take your time. Let me know when you're ready." I wasn't ready, but I knew I couldn't sit there forever. Decision time. I did have two options. Climb back down and accept defeat... or fly. I had to fly! I had no option but to fly! Especially for my husband who would have absolutely loved to experience this moment watching me be brave. He WAS watching me be brave! I was going to show him how brave I was.

Lesson number three: Being brave is not always just for you, but also for everyone watching.

Not only for those here on earth, but also for the "cloud of witnesses" cheering you on from the heavenly sidelines (Hebrews 12:1).

I was secured to the cable and given instructions, "Sit back and let the harness do its job. Just lean back, step off the platform and fly." Easy for you to say, fit and healthy 20-something-year-old that does this every day. I was scared to step off that platform. He knew that. My guide then said, "You are secure. This is a five-point harness and you are being held up by a strong cable that has been tested over and over again. It has stood the test of time and can hold weight a lot greater than yours. Just sit and let the harness hold you." Five-point harness, huh?

The number five signifies grace. I understood what God was saying in that moment.

Lesson number four: God says, "When you have no other choice but to continue on, even when you are afraid, let me hold you with my grace. You are safe in my grip. I have the strength you need. I am strong enough to carry the weight of your pain and greater. My faithfulness has withstood the test of time. I can be trusted."

Taking a deep breath I thought, "One foot in front of the other. Listen to the guide. Have faith in what he says. He's done this before. He knows what he's talking about. Follow the guide. He knows what to do, he knows where he is going and he knows how this all ends."

Lesson number five: Listen to the Sovereign Guide. He knows what He's doing, He knows where He's going and He knows how this all ends.

I sat back and stepped off. Flying through the air felt exhilarating and scary all at the same time. I screamed because that's what you're supposed to do I guess, but in that moment it was a release that I needed. I screamed out some of the fear from my guts and it felt good.

Arriving at the next platform with a slam, the instructor that had gone before me was there to catch me. I told him how my hands hurt a little bit because I was holding on so tightly. He then said, "Your hands hurt because you thought you were holding yourself up, but you weren't. The harness was doing all the work. You cannot fall. Don't hold on so tight. You can't control it. Loosen your grip and you'll be able to enjoy the ride."

Lesson number six: He's got you. Sit back, let go, and enjoy the ride.

I began to listen and obey the instructions of the guide and that's when I truly began to enjoy the adventure. Sitting back and understanding that I was not in control gave me the opportunity to look around at the beautiful scenery, laugh, and enjoy the moment.

Lesson number seven: Listen and obey the voice of the Guide for a much better experience.

Lesson number eight: Fear can blind you to the beauty along the way. Letting go of control gives you the freedom to look around and appreciate every beautiful thing around you.

I am so thankful I got to have that experience with my daughter. I am so thankful for a friend who understood what I needed. I am so thankful that Dave inspired me and I responded to God's nudges to take the first step in many adventures to come. I'll keep adventuring, as hard as it may be at times, as fear-riddled as I may become and as costly as the adventure may be, but all the while, I know my Eternal Guide and my adventurous husband will be cheering me on from Heaven. I just need to remember to look up and maybe, just maybe, I'll catch a glimpse of them smiling proudly at their girl.

Have courage. Take chances.
Try new things. Embrace adventure.
You never know what Renaissance Belle
is waiting for you on the other side of fear.

Forgiving
someone may
just be the key
you need to fly
...and be free.

Forgiveness in the Trash

———◦≈≈◦———

I t was the week before Christmas 2017, my first Christmas in 30 years without Dave. Apparently, a breaker had tripped in the garage because the refrigerator that was out there was off. I couldn't figure out what to do, so I called a friend who knows about these things and asked him. He said I needed to find a little red button that should reset the electricity in the garage. I began hunting for this little red button.

As I looked around for the reset button, I was distracted by a big black bag full of trash. It sat in a can next to the desk Dave had used so many times to draw or create his next project.

Dave had cleaned out his workshop area the week before he was transported to Heaven. There were so many things he did before leaving which makes us think, did he know? This was one of them, cleaning his workspace and throwing out things he deemed "trash."

I started to tie up the bag to pull out of the can. My intention was to put it in the large container outside. As I was taking it out of the can, I felt an impulse go through it. It was as if all of a sudden I had to see what he saw, what he touched, and what he discarded. I felt a strange compulsion to dig through this huge amount of tiny pieces of his life. I didn't really know what I was looking for.

I sat on the cold garage floor and began rummaging through the bag. Papers, old paint cans, a burnt-out light bulb, sweepings, and pieces of this and that filled the trash bag. At the very bottom, under sawdust, trash, and papers, I was surprised to find three things. I gasped and immediately heard God speak.

Before I tell you what those three things were and what God said, I must share a story that had been playing out for 26 years or so that culminates in this moment.

When we were first married, we struggled financially like most young couples do. Counting every penny each month, playing a little game called "borrowing from Peter to pay Paul." Dave worked as an art director for a company in Fort Lauderdale and getting paid very little, so he would often take freelance work to supplement our income. We were always grateful when the Art Institute recommended Dave to people looking for an artist for their projects.

One day, Dave got a phone call from a young woman who had been referred to him by the Art Institute. She was getting started on a new business idea. She wanted to produce fun toothbrushes for children in order to promote good dental hygiene habits. Sarah needed someone to design some animal characters and prototypes for her toothbrushes.

This was right up Dave's creative alley. He loved bringing an idea to fruition. We went to Sarah's apartment to meet her and hear about her business idea. She was a very nice young woman around our age, with a bubbly and friendly attitude. Her enthusiasm and excitement for her project was infectious and immediately drew us in. She described what she wanted and hired Dave for the job. He loved the challenge and went to work right away on creating some really cute designs for her. He drew a zebra, a tiger, an elephant, and an alligator dressed in human clothes.

Sarah loved and approved the artwork, and Dave began work on the prototype toothbrushes. He spent many hours sculpting each character out of clay and formed them around a simple children's toothbrush. The elephant girl wore a tutu and the alligator wore overalls. As always, I saw him do it with my own two eyes but was still amazed at how he could bring a drawing to life through sculpting.

The prototype toothbrushes turned out perfectly and the client was pleased with the work. So much so that she used them to go out and pitch her idea to interested parties. Eventually, she would use them as the prototypes for the manufacturing of the toothbrushes.

I remember going with Dave to her apartment to deliver the prototypes and collect a modest check as payment. She was "just starting out", she would tell us, so she couldn't "pay him what he was worth". Her next statement would stay with us for another 26 years: "When I make it and these are successful, I won't forget you." Then there was a "Thank you" and a handshake. Funny how people will often say things flippantly, but those same words will stay with the other person for the rest of their lives.

As two young newlyweds trying to make it in life, we believed her promise to "remember" his help in the beginning of her endeavor. On the way home, we talked about how we knew this lady would, in fact, be successful and that one day she would make it right by paying Dave what "he was worth." We were sure she wouldn't forget her promise.

In the following weeks, Dave needed to get a hold of her about something relating to the project. He called. No answer. He went to her apartment. No answer. The apartment manager told Dave that Sarah had moved and didn't leave a forwarding address or number. We had no idea what happened.

Several years later, we were living in Georgia. One day we came to realize that Sarah had indeed "made it" because we began seeing her toothbrushes in a well-known department store. Her company name was now linked to famous character branding. We were sincerely happy for her.

These were the days of AOL dialup and searching on the internet had just become a thing, so I decided to look up Sarah's company and possibly some sort of contact information. Surely she remembered her promise to my husband. It didn't take very long to find an email address for her.

My email was something like, "Hi Sarah, this is Jackie Smith from Ft. Lauderdale. David and I are so happy that your company and toothbrush idea has taken off. We live in Georgia now with our three little ones. Would love to reconnect with you." I left it at that because I wondered if she would even remember us.

Just a couple of days later, I received a response. "Of course I remember you! What's your address? I'd like to send you something." Dave and I thought it was cool that she remembered him and possibly her promise. I sent her our address. A week or so later we received a little box from Sarah. Inside were four toothbrushes. That's it. Four. Toothbrushes. We recognized these as the ones she had made from Dave's prototypes. They were adorable! Although we were actually grateful to receive the cute toothbrushes, we were bewildered. All that was in the little box were the four toothbrushes. Not even a note. In the coming years, we continued to see her company name in stores and her obvious success story. We decided to just shrug it all off and move on with life.

Fast forward 10 years or so. This is where the story gets interesting and sort of weird. It was a normal Sunday morning. We were now on staff at The Rock Family Worship Center in Huntsville, Alabama. We had just finished our first service and were getting set up to welcome kids in for the next. I stepped out into the lobby to greet kids and families. A friend of ours who owned and drove tour buses for a living happened to walk in just as I was walking out. Jerry came over and hugged me and asked how we were doing. He then said, "You should see this bus I'm driving! It's really nice. I actually have it parked out there on the far side of the parking lot. Do you want to come out and take a look?" I said, "Sure! Who are you driving for?" He responded, "I am driving a lady that has started a wig company and she is on a promotional tour. She made it big in kids' toothbrushes. Sold her company to Procter and Gamble a few years ago and made millions."

I was shocked! Could this be her? How random was it that Jerry would park his huge bus in the church parking lot on a Sunday morning and mosey on in through the children's ministry lobby and bump into me out of all the thousands of people in that building coming and going! What are the odds? Or was this a God thing? I'm sure my eyes got really big and he noticed my expression. I asked him, "Does her name happen to be Sarah?" He responded, "Yes, it is! Do you know her?" I said, "Yes, I think I do. I would love to see the bus."

My son and daughter joined me as we followed Jerry across the parking lot to the huge bus emblazoned with a picture of a woman modeling one of her wigs. My kids knew this story because they had seen the toothbrushes she had sent us about ten years prior. They always admired their dad's work and anything and everything he created. They had also seen these toothbrushes over time on the shelves of stores and knew that Dad had once helped this lady get started.

As we neared the bus and I was certain that this was, in fact, the Sarah we had often wondered what happened to, I turned to Jonny and said, "Go get your dad. Tell him there's someone out here in this bus that he needs to see. Tell him it's an old friend." In hindsight, I should have given Dave more of a heads up because when Jonny ran in with the message, he had no clue who he was going to see after all these years.

I stepped onto the bus after Jerry. He smiled and introduced me to a couple of people who would turn out to be her husband and sister who were traveling with her, and then he said, "Sarah, this is Jackie Smith. She says you guys have met before." She looked a bit bewildered while walking towards me. I said, "Hi Sarah, remember me? David and Jackie from Fort Lauderdale." She sort of turned pale and was clearly surprised to see me. She said, "Yes, of course I remember you! How are you?" and gave me a hug. I didn't know what else to say. I was trying to figure out how all this had happened. I never expected to run into her on a wig-themed tour bus in a church parking lot of all places!

We made small talk about her wigs as I waited for Dave to come out and join us. I looked out the bus window and saw him walking from the church building towards us. My poor husband was about to be thrown into an unexpected situation. He had no clue who was on that bus and why I had Jonny go get him. I realized this fact as he neared the door. I met Dave at the narrow steps and said, "It's Sarah." That's all I could get out. He said, "What?" as he stepped up into the bus.

Without hesitation, Sarah's husband, who Dave had never seen before, stood, extended his hand out and said, "So you're the guy that made my wife a millionaire!" Dave was stunned and didn't know what to say or do. Sarah came over and greeted Dave with a hug and an awkward "It's been a long time, how are you?" Dave was still frozen in his tracks trying to process what was happening. I know he was wondering why he was on this wig bus, why he was encountering this ghost from the past, and how Jerry had anything to do with it. Mumbling something about needing to get back to start the next service, Dave said goodbye and walked back through the parking lot towards the church building.

I felt bad. It didn't dawn on me that it would have been a good idea to give him some warning or the chance to decide if he even wanted to encounter Sarah again. Like a bad dream, my sweet husband probably felt like he had just stepped into a surprise party... naked.

Honestly, as we sat in his office later trying to make sense of the crazy series of events we had just lived through that morning, we agreed that neither one of us knew what to say. How do you ask for or get justice in a few seconds? Truth be told, this lady really didn't owe my husband anything. She paid him for a job he did a long time ago. Maybe her promise and handshake didn't mean to her what it meant to us. Still, I couldn't help but wonder, was this a second opportunity from God for her to keep her promise to Dave? It also makes me think now, how many times have I been given the opportunity to make things right in my own life and didn't? We never heard from her again.

Now, about 3 weeks after Dave's passing, I find myself sitting on the cold garage floor digging through a trash bag. Just rummaging and wondering all at once what I'm digging for. To my surprise, I find three adorable animal toothbrushes covered in sawdust.

As I gasped at the unexpected find, I heard God clearly say, "He forgave her. He let it go." I realized in that moment that Dave had not only thrown these relics out as a sign of closure, but he had also not told me about it. A true sign of forgiveness. He didn't need to tell me. It was between him and God. Another thought that came to mind was that God didn't need to lead me here to find this sign of forgiveness, but He chose to because He wanted me and his kids to realize Dave had forgiven and let it go before moving to Heaven. He wanted us to forgive her and let it go as well. I cleaned up these beautiful little creations, wrapped them up and gave them to my grown children for Christmas as a reminder that, just like daddy, we needed to "forgive and let it go."

This particular story about Sarah and the toothbrushes wasn't one that we talked about often and I probably wouldn't have ever mentioned it again except for the huge lesson it taught us.

Forgiveness sometimes involves action. Throwing something away, tearing something down, or maybe sending a card in the mail that says, "I forgive you." When an action is added to the posture of the heart, it somehow seals the deal.

That means you mean it and can't or shouldn't take it back. To forgive and be forgiven brings heart freedom. In this case, it not only brought freedom to Dave, but also to the closest ones to him.

I don't know what has become of Sarah or where she is today in her life's journey. I sincerely hope that she is well and that when someone hurts her heart, she is also able to forgive and let it go.

"The deeds you do may be the only sermon some persons may hear today." ~ St. Francis of Assisi

Yes, Dave, we heard you loud and clear.

Presleigh's Letter

February 24, 2018, was the 3rd month anniversary of his departure from earth. I was missing him fiercely. I needed to talk to him; tell him how I was feeling.

My mother and I sat on the living room couch. Chip and Joanna were talking about shiplap or something on the big screen on the wall. I was half paying attention and half meditating on heaven and my broken heart. Mr. and Mrs. Gaines were a terrible reminder of the sweetness of a husband and wife relationship. I didn't want to hear their cute banter, but my mom was into it. I grabbed my laptop and, finding Dave's Facebook page, I began to write him a note on his virtual wall.

The time was, 8:20 PM.

"You've been in Heaven for 3 months now...but since there's no time in eternity, I wonder if it still feels like you just got there or like you've been there forever? Either

way, I know you're having a blast! I miss you more than you could ever know, but when I think about you in God's wonderful Kingdom, I smile through my tears because I know you are so happy! One of my favorite things to think about is that you're enjoying creating without limitations! I remember your frustrations here on earth whenever you were "inventing" and couldn't find just the right material, paint color, or tool to make whatever you were making! (Although I was always amazed to watch you figure it out.) Now, you are creating with no limits, no constraints, no restraints, no boundaries! Knowing you, you are worshiping God in the throne room, then going on some sort of galactic flying adventure, then on to creating something beautiful to put in my mansion! Have fun, my love! I'll see you when it's my turn to fly. I love you forever."

Those words were a release of a little bit of pain in my heart, yet also a reminder of the hope I carry because of Jesus. I believe in a beautiful reunion to come. As I finished writing these words, I heard my cell phone buzz, alerting me to a text message. The time is significant and ties everything together. It was 9:11 pm.

Years ago I kept seeing 9:11 on morning and evening clocks. Without fail, every day when I'd glance at the phone, alarm clock, car clock, or any other clock I was around, it would be exactly 9:11. Because I believe there are no coincidences with God and that He is always speaking, I prayed and asked Him what this was about. I knew that 911 means "emergency."

I felt in my gut that God wanted me to pray about something every time I saw 911. What was the emergency He wanted me to pray about at least twice a day? Several things came to mind, but feeling like I was supposed to pray for "prodigals" remained strong on my heart.

The Bible talks about the prodigal son as one who leaves his father's home looking to make his own way, yet finds heartache instead. After a series of terrible situations and disappointments that leave him hungry and lonely, the prodigal son realizes that he was much better off in his father's house and decides to return. The story ends with the son running back into the arms of a forgiving and loving father who was waiting for him all along. There's a lot more to the story, but you'll have to read it for yourself in the book of Luke, chapter 15.

The point is that I believed God wanted me to begin praying for any prodigals that may be searching for love in all the wrong places. The ones who are searching for satisfaction, meaning, and worth in things, people, and places only to come up emptier than before. Prodigals who have somehow forgotten how much they are loved and wanted by their Heavenly Father. Since then, every time I see the numbers 911, either on a clock or anything else, I will stop what I am doing and breathe a prayer for the prodigals to remember how much they are loved and to be brave enough to come home.

Dave knew about this so whenever we were together and saw 911, he'd join me in a prayer. I remember the last morning we prayed our 9:11 prayer together. It was the day before he stepped into eternity. He was sitting in our bedroom on one of the chairs by the window. I had glanced over at the clock and of course, it said 9:11. I went over and knelt by his chair and put my hands on his lap. He held my hands in his and we prayed together "whatever it takes, Lord, bring the prodigals home." On this night in February it would be no exception. Some of the sweetest love notes have come from Heaven at exactly that time since he's been gone.

When my phone buzzed to alert me to a text that night, I noticed the time. Before reading the message, I said a quick prayer, "Lord, remember the prodigals." As I opened the text message I saw that it was from my friend, Kim. Her text included a photo of a note and a drawing by her 10-year-old daughter. It turns out Presleigh was writing a letter and drawing a picture at the very same time I had been writing the post on Dave's Facebook page that same evening.

Kim's text said, "So… Presleigh just brought this to me and felt like the Lord gave it to her. I am trying to pull it together! She knows nothing of our conversation and that you had a conversation with God asking if Dave still loved you."

Just 10 days earlier, on Valentine's Day, Kim and another friend had taken me out to brunch where I shared that I had been asking God if Dave still loved me. She had not shared this with her 10-year-old.

Presleigh's letter read, "Dear Pastor Dave and Pastor Jackie, I love y'all. Pastor Dave you have a wonder beautiful gift and Pastor Jackie I

Presleigh's Letter

Dave and I loved medieval history. Stories of jousting knights and battles fought in honor of the king. Ladies of the court, talented jesters and grand castles caught our imagination. The chivalry and romance depicted in paintings and books always captured our heart. From early in our marriage, Dave called me his lady.

I will always be his lady.

Renaissance Belle

The following poem is the 'love sonnet' I found on Dave's computer the day before Presleigh's letter.

To - **Lady** *Jacqueline the Fair*
From - *Sir David the Faithful*

> *"Car tant vous aime, sans mentir"*
> *A Medieval Sonnet by Guillaume de Machaut*
> *14th Century Italian poet[7]*

Truly, I love you so much.

Truly, that one could sooner dry up the deep sea and hold back its waves than I could constrain myself from loving you.

For my thoughts, my memories, my pleasures, and my desires are perpetually of you, whom I cannot even briefly forget.

There is no joy or pleasure or any other good that one could feel or imagine which does not seem to me worthless, whenever your sweetness sweetens my bitterness.

Therefore I adore you, I will suffer everything, experience everything, endure everything with you more than I desire any other worldly reward.

You are the true sapphire that can heal and end all my sufferings,
the diamond which brings me rejoicing,
the ruby to brighten and comfort my heart.

Presleigh's Letter

Your speech, your looks, Your bearing, make one cherish and desire all that is good, all that is right, all that is you.

Truly, I love you so much.

Captain Dave

Oh, how we loved cruising! The feeling you have after you've boarded, looked around a bit, and settled on one of the loungers with a cool drink in your hand as the ship begins to sail away is like none other. The sense that, at least for a week or so, you're leaving the hectic and stressful world behind brings immediate rest. Although like Dave and I often said, when you have a busy life and job, it takes at least a day or two to really begin to unwind.

Sailing out to the open sea with your best friend, blue sky above, turquoise waters before you, the sun shining bright, and upbeat music in the wind is the best. I only wish we had discovered this fun way to vacation much earlier in life.

Life imitates art and art imitates life…

If life is an ocean God provides for us to sail on, then our family is the vessel He gives us to live on and adventure with. Every ship has a captain and if "our" ship was our family, then my husband was the captain. He was also considered the captain of another vessel within the fleet, a vessel named Kids Quest. I was his first mate and equal partner on both, and together we sailed through beautiful waters, had tons of adventures, and weathered many a storm. Sometimes through calm waters, sometimes through rough, always searching for mysteries in the deep and looking forward to Home.

Dave and I always loved "themes" and stories to teach unforgettable lessons. God has used themes and stories to speak to my life over and over again. One of my favorite themes for our many kids' productions was "Pirates of Paradise Island." Interestingly, it was also the last one we did together in August of 2017. The message was simply that we are all sailing on the sea of life and have embarked on a journey that will take us to an eternal destination, Paradise Island. Our Great Captain, Jesus, has gone on ahead, leaving those he trusts in charge of many different jobs and positions. He's entrusted all who love Him with the great commission of inviting as many as possible to get on board the "Ecclesia," (which means church in Latin).

The ship Ecclesia, is not a church building, but the family of God. Captain Jesus directs our voyage by His Word which is both a map and a compass.

In this adventure called life, we will encounter all kinds of things. Treasure, danger, stowaways, turbulent storms, happy days, and sad ones. Celebration and joyful crew await us on any given day to make our days brighter. Every situation will teach us, and the wind of the Holy Spirit will move us forward us as our voyage steadily stays the course to our final port, Paradise Island.

Ah, Paradise Island! Our eternal Home! The one we are all sailing towards. The last time we ministered this theme of eternal life was in the city where Dave's life began, Jacksonville, Florida and at a church aptly named New LIFE Christian Fellowship.

The last song we led together on stage was, "King of My Heart". I remember singing the lyrics "You're never gonna let me down" just a little differently and intentionally that week... "You're never gonna let me *drown*." Always loving a good pun, I thought it was more appropriate with the pirate theme.

Let the King of my heart be the mountain where I run
The fountain I drink from, Oh, He is my song
Let the King of my heart be the shadow where I hide
The ransom for my life, Oh, He is my song

You are good, good, oh oh
You are good, good, oh oh
You are good, good, oh oh

You are good, good, oh oh

Let the King of my heart be the wind inside my sails
The anchor in the waves, Oh, He is my song
Let the King of my heart be the fire inside my veins
The echo of my days, Oh, He is my song

You're never gonna let, never gonna let me down.

You're never gonna let, never gonna let me drown.... [8]

Those lyrics would become so much more meaningful to me after Dave's passing. In the days and weeks following the most shocking storm we've ever lived through, one that rocked our ship violently, we wondered how we'd survive without this man at the helm. He led our family and ministry with courage, faithfulness, and strength. We never imagined His Captain and Lord would transport him to Paradise Island so soon without us.

Our son Jonathan used the ship analogy to explain how he, along with other crew members, were feeling lost on the Kids Quest ship. We had been steadily sailing towards a new adventure when the great storm shook us, and all of a sudden, we lost our captain. We were devastated.

It felt like he had just disappeared. One moment he was with us, and the next moment he was gone. Like Enoch, Captain Dave "walked faithfully with God; then he was no more because God took him away" Genesis 5:24 (NIV).

Now we found ourselves drifting in a dense fog hoping to survive and wondering how we should continue. We all held on to the mast sails for dear life trusting that God would send the breezes of His Holy Spirit to gently lead us on as He willed. Because the Lord is so personally into the details, He continued to speak in this theme to lovingly remind me that He was the One in control of our ship.

Exactly two months after Dave's transport to Paradise Island, I received a message from my friend, Holly who lives across the country. This beautiful woman had also lost a beloved husband a few years earlier. She knew of Dave's passing but had no idea about the ship and sailing theme God had been using in our conversations, thoughts, and prayers.

In her unexpected message, she said, "I just wanted to propose a wild invitation. I'm flying to Sydney (Australia) on Sunday, March 11th, for the Colour Conference. The theme this year is "Wind in Her Sails." I know what it feels like to have the wind knocked out of your sails and I know you do too." She continued, "I love this conference theme. It goes well with the painting I have over my fireplace. When I was struggling with the idea of moving to Seattle I played the song 'Captain,' often to remind myself that I really do believe every word of this." With her message, she included a photo of the framed picture she was referencing… not surprisingly, it was a beautiful sailing ship rocking in the ocean waves. Wow! The Lord had communicated once again in a very specific way.

In her message, Holly also included the lyrics to "Captain". This song quickly became my companion and prayer.

Renaissance Belle

"Captain"

Through waters uncharted my soul will embark
I'll follow Your voice straight into the dark
And if from the course You intend I depart
Speak to the sails of my wandering heart

Like the wind , You'll guide
Clear the skies before me, And I'll glide this open sea
Like the stars, Your word
Will align my voyage
And remind me where I've been
And where I am going

Lost in the shallows amidst fear and fog
Your truth is the compass, That points me back north
Jesus, my Captain - My soul's trusted Lord
All my allegiance is rightfully Yours

Like the wind, You'll guide
Clear the skies before me, And I'll glide this open sea
Like the stars, Your word
Will align my voyage
And remind me where I've been
And where I am going

Like the wind, You'll guide
Clear the skies before me, And I'll glide this open sea
Like the stars, Your word
Will align my voyage
And remind me where I've been
And where I am going

Jesus, my captain - My soul's trusted Lord
All my allegiance is rightfully Yours[9]

I took my friend up on her invitation and went on that wild adventure to Sydney, Australia. Just four months after Dave's passing I found myself on a trip to the other side of the world all by myself because God told me to "say yes to adventure." That would be the first of many adventures to come. Heavenly "love notes" were sprinkled throughout the entire trip, God's beautiful reminders that He was very present with me in this journey to the other side of the world.

The week at the Colour Conference was wonderful. I was encouraged, uplifted, and felt life breathed into me. Through the conference theme, "Wind in Her Sails," God spoke to me over and over in so many ways.

Right at the beginning of the conference, the lead pastor read the following poem from the stage. (I have taken the liberty of changing the "she" to "he" so you can see why it so impacted me.)

"Gone From My Sight"

I am standing upon the seashore.

A ship at my side
spreads its white sails to the moving breeze and starts
for the blue ocean. He is an object of beauty and strength.
I stand and watch him until, at length, he hangs like a speck
of white cloud just where the sea and sky come to mingle with
each other.

Then, someone at my side says, "There, he is gone."

Gone where?

Gone from my sight. That is all. He is just as large in mast,
hull and spar as he was when he left my side.
And, he is just as able to bear his load of living freight to his
destined port.

His diminished size is in me -- not in him.

And, just at the moment when someone says, "There, he is gone,"
there are other eyes watching him coming, and other voices
ready to take up the glad shout, "Here he comes!"

And that is dying... [10]

I wonder if my heart will continue to beat.
I wonder how I'm going to live without him.
I wonder if I can survive this.
I wonder how my children will be able to live without their dad.
I wonder why this happened.
I wonder what I'm going to do now.
I wonder who I am.
I wonder what's going to happen with our ministry.
I wonder if he knew he was going to die.

I was full of "wonder" as in questioning. Then I quickly became full of wonder in a supernatural way. I realized that Dave had done so many things to prepare for his departure. I saw God's hand in the way He took him from this earth. I remembered that I heard him fly out of his body. It was all so tragic and "wonder-full" all at the same time.

I began to think about our story, our life, our love, and how wonderful it was. I thought about how he called me his Wonder Woman and I wondered now if I could live up to his beautiful expectation of me. *Yes, he always described me as a "wonder woman," yet now I was suddenly a "widowed woman."*

"Widow? Me?"

I understand that the Bible talks so beautifully about the way God loves widows and becomes their husband. It also admonishes others to take care of widows, especially older ones. But in all honesty, I don't like the fact that I am one. I never imagined I'd be one! I feel like I was thrust into this position too quickly and without permission… an uninvited "suddenly."

A "widow" in my mind had always described an elderly woman with silken white hair. She would have lived 50 plus long years married to a beloved husband who is now a "dearly departed". Wearing a long black dress and veil, she sits on a rocking chair all day waiting for her turn to join him in the clouds. She lives sad and alone. In my mind, that was the caricature I had always associated with the word "widow." I know, I know. Kind of ridiculous and dramatic, especially since I personally have known many widows who do not fall under that description at all.

Now, here I was, just 51 years old and a "widow". I didn't want to hear the word, especially in those terrible first days. Sadly, just three days after Dave passed, at his life celebration, a couple of ladies who meant well decided to ask me to join them at their "widow's ministry." I couldn't believe it! I couldn't believe they would stand in the very long line to greet me at the front of the church auditorium where I stood with my grieving children simply to hug me and say, "We oversee the widow's ministry and want you to come to one of our meetings." I thought I would faint. Those words hit me like a ton of bricks and made my knees buckle. If it weren't for a friend who sat behind me, literally holding me up, I would have crumbled right there and then. I know those ladies didn't mean to harm my heart in any way. I just think their good intentions were ill-timed.

A word of advice, don't address a newly widowed woman as a widow, she's just not ready for it, especially if she's young and her husband's passing was unexpected. She already knows it. She knew it the moment her husband left this earth. Please don't remind her. As a matter of fact, as I told countless people who came to hug and greet me as we gathered to say goodbye to Dave, "You are exempt from having to find the right words to say. There are no words that can make me feel any better. None. I release you from feeling an obligation to find comforting words."

The worst thing that happens in these moments is that people who mean well feel like they need to say something, anything, to fill uncomfortable space. My advice is use few words or none at all. Just hug the person and tell them you love them. Cry with them. Listen to them talk about their beloved. Hold their hand. Give practical support and help. Hand them a tissue or water. Make them food. But don't use many words. This is the moment where silence is golden.

As of this writing, I personally know nineteen friends or friends of friends who have been given the unpleasant distinction of wearing this label and being a member of this most undesired club.

Some of these ladies had a "heads up" because their husbands became sick. Some of us didn't have a clue. Either way, it's an awful bucket of cold water straight to the heart. You are left numb. In shock. Not knowing what the next step is.

Although we share the common bond of widowhood and we can relate in many ways, each of our stories is different and unique. Just as unique as each of us are. Just as unique as each marriage relationship we were in was. No matter how long they were married or the particular relationship they shared with their spouse, there will be grief.

Whether they had the blessing of a fairytale marriage, a nightmare relationship, or somewhere in between, there will be intense pain regardless. They are missing the dreams they got to live or the ones they never had fulfilled with the man that is now gone. Whether there are beautiful memories of many or few years together or maybe sad regrets of days spent in a lonely marriage. All of a sudden, you're turning the page on a new chapter. What is past no one can change. Good, bad, or indifferent, it's a vapor in the wind. Behind lies all the things that were… or hopes of things that could have been. Memories are all that's left.

We cannot undo or recreate the past. But we can help build the future that is ahead of us. Not that it's completely in our hands as to how our story ends, but we can certainly have a say in the attitude and outlook we bring with us as we walk ahead in this new road.

Whether slowly, tentatively, reservedly, or begrudgingly, we must walk forward into our future.

The story we've lived so far was no accident. For better or for worse, as most vows go, we lived through it. In sickness and in health, we were there for our husbands. Now we stand alone, although at times surrounded by loved ones and friends, still alone in a dream that was cut short. Alone in bed at night as we fall asleep. When we awake, we're still alone. Those two times are the loneliest moments of the day.

Some of these women will move on ahead to find that God has a new love for them to share life with. A brand new start with a prince that awaits his dream girl. Some of us will walk alone whether by choice or by chance until we are reunited with the one we said goodbye to on this side of Heaven.

Whatever the case, the Lord has seen fit to give us this journey. He must have seen strength in us we never knew was there. Maybe it wasn't so much our own strength, but the supernatural strength God knew we'd grab onto. His strength.

As I ponder on all these women around me who have lost their husbands, I pray out loud, "God, what are you doing? Are you assembling an army of Wonder Women on earth?" In my imagination, I saw God gathering a tribe of strong, powerful, and brave Wonder Women who have acquired their supernatural strength through an otherworldly encounter with their supernatural God. A unique encounter that can only be had when half of you has been taken away and all you have left is complete and utter trust in the One who holds you together. This is a distinct group of lady fighters who couldn't make it without their Soul Provider. A courageous bunch who somehow will do amazing things even through their pain, tears, and grief.

These warrior women have looked death in the face, their hearts ripped out from their chests, and yet are still able to declare a future filled with hope for themselves and their children. Their anthem is "Even though I walk through the valley of the shadow of death, I will fear no evil for YOU are with me!" Through the tears. Through the darkest of nights.

Through the loneliest of days. They stand strong, ready to take on whatever comes their way. There will be no retreat into the depths of despair because the Lord God is their King.

They have Holy Spirit as their Great Comforter and Jesus their closest friend. These Wonder Women rely wholly on the One who loves them most. These strong and brave ones will carry on with grace and dignity.

This tribe has the potential to do great things on the earth, especially if they band together and unite their strengths and talents. Going about doing good, saving the lost, consoling the grieving, and encouraging the weak. Their superpowers come from an unseen realm where their heart lives on. Looking back only to gather resolve- knowing what their beloved would say, "Keep going, don't give up; you are stronger, braver, and smarter than you ever knew!" Standing strong in the face of the unknown. Fighting fear and combating the urge to withdraw from the battle, moving forward one step at a time… sometimes one breath at a time, but always moving forward. These women are the Wonders among us!

On the day of my first birthday without Dave, my daughter and I were at the grocery store. As we walked through the coffee aisle, a really unique mug caught Britt's eye. After looking at it intently, she said, "Mom, you need this!" The mug was covered in sketches of Wonder Woman in all kinds of fighting stances and brave poses. Wonder Woman looked fierce and ready for battle in all the images around that mug, but what caught Britt's eye was the one drawing that was the only one not duplicated and neither of us had ever seen before. Right in the middle of all the amazingly brave poses, Wonder Woman is drawn on her knees, head bowed with a daisy in her hand. She is pulling a petal off of the flower as if reciting the old child's game phrase, "Love me. Love me not."

This demeanor is one that I have never seen this Amazonian character portrayed in. Wonder Woman is known for her strength, power, and bravery, yet here, in the midst of her power poses, she is surprisingly vulnerable and deep in thought about whether her beloved still loves and thinks of her. We found it interesting that this mug seemed to reflect my journey. Yes, I have been strong and brave, but also sentimentally vulnerable in the midst of it all. In my weakest moments, I have gathered strength from a supernatural place on my knees. Wondering the "why" of all of this, yet unwavering in faith, I have asked if I am still loved by my husband.

I have found that the answer is a most certain "Yes! He loves you more than ever and can't wait to be reunited with his Wonder Woman." I knew this mug was a heavenly love note on my birthday… and if you're wondering… of course, I bought the mug.

Dedicated to all the ladies who have learned to live as Wonders among us.

You think she's weak but there's a lion underneath.
Just watch her go as she starts to bear her teeth...
And roar like thunder,
Roar like the ocean's waves,
Roar like she's unafraid!

With every new beginning, there are
so many choices to be made...
Choose to be brave, even when you can't
see what the whole picture looks like...

Choose to walk forward, one step at a time...

Choose to make new memories
and not forget the old...

Choose to embrace each day
with hope and faith...

Choose to trust even through the tears...

Each choice will get you closer to your
Renaissance Belle!

I Am Kintsugi

———◦⌘⌘◦———

Kintsugi or Kintsukuroi poetically translates as "golden joinery" or "golden repair". This is the ancient Japanese art of repairing broken pottery with a special lacquer resin dusted or mixed with powdered gold, silver, or platinum. The philosophy is that a vessel's breakage or damage should be displayed and shown as part of the piece's history, rather than something to be disguised. The thought is that a broken piece of pottery should not be discarded simply because it's been damaged, but should and can be restored into a work of art.

If you have never experienced truly being broken, just wait; at some point in life, you will. Whether you have been in the past, are currently walking in a state of brokenness, or will be broken in the future, I have good news. Right in the middle of your shattered state of being, God wants to show you purpose. He never discards broken people. **With God nothing is wasted, not even our pain.**

Whether your heart has been shattered due to the death of a loved one, abuse, rejection, loss of a job, divorce, or disillusionment of a dream that could have and should have been, there's hope. You're never too broken that God cannot pick up your pieces and put you back together. You may not look the same. As a matter of fact, you won't ever look the same! Be sure of this though: you will survive. There is still worth in your existence. There are still useful pieces and parts of your story that must be put together to form a beautiful picture. It's not over. You're not done. He's not done with you. As long as you have breath, there is still more to your story.

You may ask, "How can something that is broken ever be beautiful?" I asked myself this question after the shattering of my own life. In the early morning hours of November 24, 2017, in an instant, I was broken into a million pieces. How can I go on living? How in the world can I survive this? These were my first thoughts as I shook awake from the shock. I could not imagine my life without my husband. I felt I could not even breathe, walk, or function in those first few days, yet there was a powerful force greater than my humanity carrying me. All of a sudden the Scriptures I had believed, quoted, and taught for 40 years came to life. The "peace that passes understanding" was REAL and DID pass all understanding because in the midst of this tragedy there was supernatural peace that I could not understand.

"The Lord is close to the brokenhearted" was true. I felt Him so near. So close I could see Him in everyone that came to offer a hug, a tear, or a meal. I could sense His arms around me. I literally felt His hand on my shoulder during a particularly dark moment of grief. "My grace is sufficient" all of a sudden made sense like never before. As long as I had His grace resting on me, I could stand. His grace caused me to stand for hours hugging and greeting people at my husband's life celebration. I could have never imagined that I would be able to before this all happened.

Supernatural grace.   *Heavenly presence.*

I could have never imagined feeling this broken. The hours, days and months progressed. Treacherously slow at times. In the agonizing long days and dark, lonely nights without my husband, full of tears and questions… still God remained near. So near in fact, that each day, strength that I never thought possible has been my sustenance. I was shattered to pieces and felt crushed under the load of grief and daily decisions that had to be made without him and about him. Every time I had to show the death certificate to authenticate my husband's passing was a dagger through my heart. It was like I had to relive the fact that he was really gone. The small box that sits on my bedroom dresser reminds me daily that his body was reduced to ashes.

All the "firsts" without him were so very difficult… the first trip to get groceries, the first walk around the neighborhood, the first church service, the first trip to Disney World, the first Christmas, New Year, birthday, Valentine's, and anniversary, all without the one person I had shared it all with for 32 years. Even the birth of our first grandbaby, one of the happiest days of my life, was also bittersweet. I have prayed every morning asking Him for His strength, for His grace to see me through. I've asked

God for His guidance in every decision. Of course, I had always turned to the Lord to lead me; to lead us, but at that time, I had my husband to lean on, to inquire of, to get an opinion from, and to make decisions with.

Now that is gone. It's just me and God. This is the hardest thing I've ever walked through. I am broken. I have struggled to understand how God could possibly put these pieces back together again. I know He can. He is God. He can do anything. Nothing is impossible for Him. I believe that with all my heart, but wow, this is a mess. My heart is in a million pieces.

Life is fragile. Now I know that more than ever. The Bible says that our life is like a withering flower and we are but dust.

> *For he knows we are but dust and that our days are few and brief, like grass, like flowers, blown by the wind and gone forever.*
>
> *—Psalm 103:14-16 TLB*

Recalling back to Genesis where God created man from the dust of the earth, we are reminded that yes, we are just clay. When God formed Adam out of dust, He then breathed INTO him His very breath. "Then the LORD God formed a man from the dust of the ground and breathed into his nostrils the breath of life, and the man became a living being." Genesis 2:7 (NIV)

God filled the first man with Himself, His essence, and His very Ruach. To inspire is to breathe into. God inspired man. We are vessels made of clay. We are made to be containers. Containers of His breath. We can then say that God is our greatest inspiration in and of life. So when we say, "I am inspired by God" we can equate that to being breathed into by the very Creator to be able to create!

As clay vessels, however, we can be broken. One day in worship at church, not long after losing Dave, I raised my hands in surrender and whispered to God, "I love you, but I am so broken." Immediately, I heard Him respond to my spirit, *"I validate your brokenness."* He was saying He SAW me in my current state of brokenness and He understood I was hurting. This meant the world to me at that moment. My Heavenly Father sees me and does not discard my pain. He cared about how much pain my broken heart was feeling.

He continued speaking to my heart, "Everyone goes through brokenness. Some by accident, some by disobedience, some by carelessness, and others by abuse. There's one other way people are broken. Sometimes it's on purpose... for purpose." Immediately I thought, "Lord, I understand the ways we can be broken and damaged by accident, disobedience, carelessness, and abuse, but what do you mean "on purpose for purpose?" Before my question had been formed and as fast as lighting He answered, *"Like a glow stick."* He continued, *"A glow stick won't achieve its purpose without being broken. It is meant to be broken on purpose for purpose. It's broken to shine."*

Purpose: the reason for which something is done or created or for which something exists.[13]

Ah!

On purpose.

With purpose.

For purpose.

A glow stick is simply a dull, plastic container with liquid color before its intended use. Only after the shaking and breaking does it fulfill its purpose. We all have purpose. We're all on this earth for a reason. We all get broken. We all bear scars of breakage.

Just like the carefully repaired cracks on pottery in the art of kintsugi, our scars are there to show what we've been through. A scar is a reminder of a mending, meaning that what was once broken, has now healed. Mended. It's a reminder of the pain and what caused it, but it's also a reminder that with time, attention, and purposeful care, broken things can be mended. Does it happen overnight? Not usually. Sometimes it takes a long time for a wound to heal. Whether it's your physical body or your heart. Sometimes it takes years for a scar to be the only thing left to remind you of the pain of your past.

As a child, I fell many times and scraped my knees. My small bleeding wound would later create a scab. As the natural progression of healing begins, a scab forms to protect what's underneath from outside sources, germs, and dirt. I was ignorant of the fact that I had to "leave it alone and let it heal." As most kids do, I often picked at my scabs opening them back up and causing them to bleed. I didn't know that by doing this, there was the potential of getting the wound infected, making it take longer to heal, and possibly leaving a bigger scar. My childish ignorance and curiosity would hinder the healing process, but I didn't know it.

While a wound is healing it sometimes looks terrible. We tend to want to "help it along" by messing with it, not understanding that it will look gross for just a little while. In its present state of going through the process of healing, it does not look like what it will look like after it's healed. When our hearts, feelings, emotions, and bodies are broken and we are just beginning to walk through the healing process, we tend to want to pick at the wound. While it's healing, we should let forgiveness, hope, and patience be allowed to do their job.

Instead as humans, we tend to relive the experience over and over in our minds, picking at the scab, allowing words of bitterness to play over and over like a scratched record. We meditate on the words spoken, the terrible actions that hurt us so deeply, making the scab bleed again and again. We often delay the process of healing, making the wound bigger, promoting additional unnecessary scarring. The more we pick at it, the longer it will take to heal. In our childish ignorance or stubbornness, we don't understand that if we allow God to use His methods of healing, the process will be quicker and the scar won't be as prominent.

Does this mean that we ignore the gaping wound that a careless word, selfish motive, or hateful action has caused? No, not at all. Tending to a real wound is important and should not be ignored. The pain is real. The hurt is real. The cut is real. It needs to be dealt with. It needs to be looked at and validated. The proper medicine should be applied, Going to God in prayer is essential; oftentimes we may even need help in the way of therapy and counseling.

I'm not a nurse, but as a mom, I knew that the first thing I needed to do when my kids ran in from a fall off their bike with some sort of scrape or cut, was to look at it. I had to validate their pain. I had to stop what I was doing and determine what the next action should be. Sometimes it was a small, very temporary boo-boo that simply needed love, attention, and a kiss. For some hurts, that's all it takes, running to Daddy and saying, "Lord, this careless word by my friend hurt me. I know they didn't mean to hurt me, but it did. Here it is. Would you kiss it and make it better?" He will. This kind of hurt could potentially happen every day.

As toddlers, sometimes my kids would come up to me with imaginary boo-boos simply because they wanted my attention. As little ones without maturity, they thought they were pulling one over on me. Since they were little and lacked understanding in many ways, I played along with a wink to the other adults in the room and kissed their "boo boo" and sent them on their way. Immediately after getting the attention they wanted, they ran off to play with smiles and giggles. As their understanding grew, when there was a minimal hurt, after assessing and determining that they didn't really hurt themselves and in order to teach them, I began to say, "You're ok, it didn't hurt that bad," maybe rubbing it a little bit to show them how quickly the pain would go away.

At different times in their growing up years they would run in with scrapes and cuts, I would say, "Let's clean that up," taking care to clean off the obvious outside factors that could infect it or make it worse. Sometimes a little bit of water on a paper towel and a Band-Aid would do the trick. On other occasions, the injury might require some hydrogen peroxide, antibiotic ointment, and a bandage. Depending on the particular situation, after validation and attention, the proper care needed to be applied. The deeper the cut or wound, the more care and attention it might require. At times even a trip to the emergency room for stitches might be in order. A broken bone would require even more attention and care with a cast or even surgery.

God knows the level of our hurt and brokenness. He gives us the validation that a good Father does to a child who runs in crying and asking Him for help. "Daddy, I'm hurt and I need you to look at it," and understand. Oftentimes, He will kiss it and send you on your way. There have been many times that I ran to Him with an exaggerated "hurt" or offense and He responded with, "Ok, I see you, I love you, but you need to let that go. It's not that bad. Forgive and move on; you'll be just fine."

As I grew up in spiritual maturity, I learned to determine what kind of attention was required for different hurts, wounds, and offenses. I began to understand that some things were just not worth my time, attention, and tears. I learned to let go of offense quickly and move on to more important things that required true attention. There have also been bigger situations in life that were deeper cuts. Hurts that required God to perform surgery. Pain that only He could heal. You may be broken or damaged but in God's hands, redemption, restoration, repurposing, and renewal are possible. Whether your vessel's breakage is minimal or extensive, He can take all those broken pieces and put them back together, adhering them with value and worth.

God's care and love can make kintsugi out of you.

My heart has been broken. It will slowly heal with time, but I know it will bear a deep scar. That scar will forever remind me of my greatest loss on this earth. I will never get "over" this great loss, but I will learn to live with it. I will learn to cope in spite of it. I will learn to move forward with it near and dear to me. Tears will always accompany my memories of the greatest love story I have ever known. When a word or a thought touches that scar, I will remember the pain.

If you find yourself a broken vessel, I encourage you to give the Master Potter all the pieces. He knows exactly how to put you back together again. He is in the business of re-purposing broken vessels. It may not happen over night, but you can be sure that the finished result will be of great worth and part of a story worth telling.

"Yet you, LORD, are our Father. We are the clay, you are the potter; we are all the work of your hand."

—Isaiah 64:8 NIV

I Am Kintsugi

May the wisdom in the art of kintsugi be a
reminder that broken can be beautiful.

I have changed.

I will never be the same.

I will bear my gold-filled scars
        proudly as they have cost much
and the story is worth telling.

I am Kintsugi.

Love Notes and Miracle Moments

——— ⟡ ———

T hroughout my life, I have tried to remain sensitive to God's presence and watch for Him in every situation and in the smallest of details. Like I have mentioned multiple times, there have been many unique, inexplicable moments especially in this latest part of my journey. The only way I can describe these experiences is that they are snippets in time where Heaven's reality touches mine. I call these my heavenly "love notes".

Some I will keep close to my heart and share only with those closest to me, others I have already shared within these pages.

Here are a few more "love notes" I'd like to share with you.

A Love Letter to Heaven

The first Christmas after Dave passed was so hard! Looking back I know that the only way we got through it was with God's strength. If we could have heard Dave say anything to us it would have been that we could not let this season go by without putting up a tree, hanging some lights and wrapping a few gifts. He would have added that the meaning of this holiday had not changed simply because he had changed his address. Some wonderful family members came over and helped me take down Thanksgiving decorations and put up Christmas

ones. We made sure to display his Captain America Christmas tree in a prominent place.

It was a couple of days before Christmas. I had gone shopping by myself to purchase some Christmas gifts for the family. This day turned out to be very difficult, full of errands that I had to muster up the strength for. By the evening, I was tired and emotionally spent. Tears and tears flowed as I drove to the last store. I decided that I would send Dave a letter. I know that sounds crazy, but in that moment it made so much sense. Praying out loud I said, "God, there's so much I want to say to Dave right now. Please send me a scribe angel to write down my words. I would like for it to be on a scroll and in gold writing, please. I'll wait." I paused imagining the scribe angel being requested to fly down to my car, gold quill feather pen in hand and a long scroll (because I had a lot to say).

I began to dictate my letter: "Sweetheart, I miss you so much! We are all feeling so lost without you. There are not enough words to express how my heart aches. We only had 32 years together. I wanted another 32. It just wasn't enough." I went on and on, my heart pouring out my deepest pain and my eyes pouring out liquid love. I finished with my dictation with, "Don't worry about us. We are going to be okay. I know the Lord will give us the strength we need to live this life without you. Until we're together again, have fun! Enjoy your adventures with Jesus. I know you'll be planning some good ones for when I get there. I'll love you forever." In my mind's eye, I imagined the scribe angel ready to hand the rolled up scroll to the courier angel for delivery. All of a sudden I said, "Oh, wait! I want to add one more thing…. P.S. I expect an answer." I didn't really think much about my P.S. before it came out of my mouth. It was just a blurting out of faith and hope that somehow Dave would "write me back."

I felt relieved and satisfied that I had gotten a lot off my chest in this love letter to Heaven. I was sure it was in the hands of the courier angel on the way to Dave's mansion because I believe what Jesus said, "With man this is impossible, but with God all things are possible." (Matthew 19:26 NIV)

That same night I received an answer.

On this first Christmas without their dad, I decided my kids needed to receive some significant gifts from him. I stepped into Dave's walk-in closet looking for some items that would be meaningful for our kids. I was determined that there would be treasures under the tree.

I opened the closet door and looked around. Not really sure what I was looking for, I glanced up to a shelf. That's when I noticed something sitting at the very back corner. It was a small cylinder with a bow on it. I had never seen it before. After several attempts, I was able to reach it. Apparently it had been up there for a very long time because it was a bit dusty. I wondered what this little container would reveal. I opened the top and found a small scroll with vinyl letters that read, "Just one lifetime won't be enough

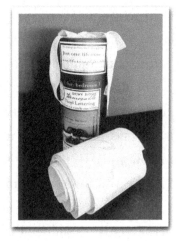

for us." Wow! There it was. The answer I prayed and hoped for in the very moment I needed it! And on a scroll no less! One lifetime was not enough, so thankful we will have eternity.

My Red Coat

The very next day I had to go somewhere for something. I really didn't want to. It was just two days before Christmas. I was so weighed down by sadness. December had brought with it bleak, cold and grey skies. I remember thinking that the weather was a perfect reflection of my grief. As I reached for my black winter coat I commented to my mother that I wished for a bright red coat. Red has always been my favorite color. Grabbing my black pea coat from the closet that afternoon made me imagine that wearing a red one instead would somehow brighten this impossible situation I found myself in. I left that passing thought behind as we moved on with our errands.

It was late into the night by the time I was wrapping the last of the gifts and I remembered there were a few more of Dave's things I wanted to wrap as gifts for the kids. Going back into his closet something new caught my eye. At the very back of the closet behind dozens of shirts, I could see black fur. The fur caught my attention and I remember thinking, "That's weird, Dave doesn't have anything with fur on it." As I moved the hangers aside I was shocked to see a beautiful, bright red coat with black buttons and fur! The prettiest red coat I had ever seen! So many thoughts and emotions went through me all at once. I had been in this closet many times since his passing. How did I not see this before? The coat still had creases from being folded and I guessed it was because it had come in a delivery package. Dave had hung it in his closet to loosen the creases. He hid it where he knew I would not look for it. All the questions bounced in my mind. When had he purchased this? Where did he find this? How long has it been in his closet? That's when I realized that it was my Christmas gift and that he was saving it to give it to me… today! Looking at the clock I realized that it was now after midnight. It was Christmas Eve!

I slowly pulled the coat out of its hiding place, still bewildered and amazed. I slipped it on and looked in the long mirror. How could I not smile? It fit perfectly! I got my wish. A beautiful, bright red coat for Christmas… from my husband.

To this day I have not been able to figure out how or where Dave bought my coat. I have searched and searched through all our accounts without a trace of the purchase. I love my miracle red coat.

Love Is Forever

In the first few murky days of living with the realization that Dave was gone and that now he was living in another reality without me, all I could think of was, "Does he still love me?" Even though I had experienced the passing of other people I cared about, I had never really thought about how they felt about me while continuing their existence on the other side. Now it was more personal than ever and extremely important for me to know if the life of love we shared on this side of Heaven continued on the other side. That night I fell asleep crying, asking the Lord, "Does Dave still love me?"

My broken heart had to know. The very next day was going to be my first Sunday back to church and the children's ministry we had built together. Stepping in to the Kids Quest area that morning was so difficult. I thought my heart would fall right out of my chest and shatter on the floor. A couple who had been our right hand ministry assistants for years were handling the children's service. I was able to stand before the kids that morning and speak to them briefly. I remember telling them that Pastor Dave had gone to Heaven and that we would all miss him very much, but one day we would be together again. My tears began to flow and I consciously allowed myself to feel all of the pain in my heart on that familiar stage. Many children cried with me, others sort of sat and stared sadly. I explained to them that it was okay to cry and express the emotion in our hearts at a time like this. Tears are liquid love and sometimes they spill out from the overflow of your heart.

After talking to the kids for just a couple of minutes I made my way backstage. Deep, heartfelt hugs were exchanged and more tears were shed with our young adult and teen leaders. They were all heartbroken and didn't know what to say. Words did not need to be uttered. I could see it in their eyes and feel it in their embrace. Most of those young adults had been in our ministry since they themselves were little ones. They had learned about Heaven from Pastor Dave who now was there himself. It was a very emotional morning.

As I sat backstage, I inhaled deeply thinking about all the times Dave and I found ourselves in this very spot preparing to step out to teach a lesson. I then exhaled intentionally, knowing this was the last time I would sit in this familiar spot. In that moment a young lady named Lauren walked over and sat next to me. She whispered, "Can I tell you something?" I said, "Yes, of course".

Lauren told me that she had a dream. In her dream she saw Pastor Dave sitting in the room backstage like he always did on Sunday mornings. Lauren said that she was shocked and excited to see him again. She said, "I have so many things I want to ask you." Dave looked at her and said, "I need you to do something for me."

He continued, "Tell Pastor Jackie that I love her. Can you do that?" Lauren responded to him with a certain, "Yes, sir". Then he added, "Also tell her to find the letter I wrote".

As Lauren relayed her dream, I was in sweet shock. I knew this was God allowing Dave himself to answer the question that burned in my heart the night before, "Does he still love me?"

What an amazing message this was to me! Our loved ones on the other side of the invisible veil do think about us and do love us. Probably more than they ever had the capacity to love us here on earth. I wondered about this letter he said I needed to find. There was no doubt in my mind there was a letter somewhere that had something I needed to read. In the following days I looked everywhere. In his computer, closet, drawers and every pocket. Nothing. I remember thinking, "Okay I know I'll find it in the moment I need it". Then I just let it go.

A few weeks later, on Valentine's Day eve, I sat in my closet and wept bitterly. The thought that I would never hear him call me his "Spanish Princess" again broke my heart all over again. I felt the weight of grief sitting on my chest. All of a sudden I glanced up to a shoebox on a shelf. "There it is! The letter is in there" I thought. I don't know how I knew it. I just did. Nervously I reached up and grabbed the box. In my mind, I did not know what was in there, but in my heart I knew the letter Dave told Lauren I had to find would be in there. I opened the box slowly. Inside I found a letter Dave had written to me several years before while I attended a spiritual renewal weekend. It had been in this box since then. As I opened the envelope I knew this was the letter he wanted me to find and these would be the words he wanted me to hear in this moment...and he starts by calling me his Spanish princess. Amazing!

One Sock at a Time

Today I struggle as I try to wrap this up. Writing my story and deciding to share it with others has been a journey in and of itself. How do I now 'finish' something that still continues every day? So many thoughts. So many emotions. How do I say "The End" to a story that has no end? What will people think? Will anyone care to read my words?

I feel anxious. More anxious than many other anxious times in my life.

I think to myself, *What would Dave say to me right now?* His advice would be something practical and creative. Yes, I know what he would say. If he were right here, right now, he would tell me exactly what he told me on so many other occasions when fear tried to overwhelm and paralyze me and I didn't know what to do.

"One sock at a time."

I'll never forget the time he came up with this piece of clever advice. That particular afternoon I was feeling anxious and upset thinking about my long to-do list. There were so many things pulling at me and demanding my attention. I couldn't get my thoughts straight. Even something as silly as the big mountain of laundry that needed folding looked like Kilimanjaro to me. I just stood in the middle of our bedroom, frozen, tears rolling down my face.

Dave came over to me, wrapped his arms around me, and kissed me on top of my head. I cried into his chest, "I have so much to do". He held me and gently spoke the words that to this day reverberate in my mind every time I find myself in this same life predicament. He said, "Sweetheart, everything is going to be ok. Do you see that big pile of laundry on the bed that needs folding? I know it looks like a big task. Do you know how you are going to get through it?"

Crying, I responded, "I don't know." Dave said, "One sock at a time. First, you're going to find a sock. That's it. Just one sock. Then, you'll look for and find the matching sock. You'll put them together, fold them, and set them aside. That's it. One task is done. Then you'll go on to the next sock. That's exactly how you are going to tackle all these responsibilities before you. One sock at a time. Figure out the one 'sock' that requires immediate attention. Do that. Then, move on to the next sock. Okay? Now breathe…. One sock at a time."

So much wisdom. So much patience. He was my gift from God. From that day on, I began to apply this very simple philosophy to daunting tasks before me and it has really helped.

"One sock at a time."

So… wrapping this up IS my one sock at hand.

My life seemed so ordinary while I was living it, but now looking back I realize that it was actually extraordinary. Not many get to say they lived such a wonderful love story. Not many get to say they were loved so well. Every love story may be beautiful, but truly ours is my favorite.

Since I still find myself breathing on this side of Heaven, I guess my story is not over. I'm sure I'll have many more stories to share. Many more memories to make.

I choose to believe and walk out the words found in Psalm 27:13 and 14 which I have paraphrased for myself, "I would have despaired and fainted if I had not believed, trusted and remained confident in this, I will see the goodness of the Lord in the land of the living. I will wait for the Lord, I will be strong and I will take heart… and wait on the Lord to accomplish His purpose in me."

I will continue to walk out the journey set before me. I will embrace every Renaissance Belle. I will say "yes" to adventure. I will keep loving those around me. I will keep looking for God and His goodness in every detail. I will appreciate every single love note from Heaven.

That's what my Dave would want me to do…. until our love story continues on the other side.

I believe with all of my heart in love ever after.

"Oh, Aslan," said Lucy.
"Will you tell us how to get into your
country from our world?"

"I shall be telling you all the time," said Aslan.
"But I will not tell you how long
or short the way will be;
only that it lies across a river.

But do not fear that, for
I am the great Bridge Builder." [14]

When the DAY comes for ONE
of us to go on AloNE, I want the
memory & the hope of seeing Each other
face to face Again to Be the STRENGTH
to help us go on.

Yes, Sweetheart,
I'll see you again soon...

Permissions

1. Page 121 | "Worth It All" Copyright © 2002 Worship Together Music (BMI) (adm. at CapitolCMGPublishing.com) All rights reserved. Used by permission.

2. Page 128 | "Stars & Galaxies" Written by Payton Pruitt, Performed by Carver Commodore ©2017 Tridents of Florence Music. Used by permission.

3. Page 141 | "Beyond the Sea" by Charles Trenet and Albert Lasry English lyric by Jack Lawrence. Used with kind permission of Pompidou Music (ASCAP) c/o Lipservices and Round Hill Music. All rights reserved. International copyright secured.

4. Page 143, 144 | "Heaven's Shore" (Forevermore) So Essential Tunes (SESAC) / Hipgnosis Songs Essential (SESAC) / (admin at EssentialMusicPublishing.com [3]). All rights reserved. Used by permission.

5. Page 145 | "You're Beautiful" © 2007 Phil Wickham Music (BMI)/ Seems Like Music (BMI)/Sing My Songs (BMI) (all rights admin. by BMG Rights Management c/o Music Services). All rights reserved. Used by permission.

6. Page 173 | Captain America Quote: J. Michael Straczynski, The Amazing Spider-Man: Civil War

7. Page 210 | Guillaume de Machaut "Car tant vous aime, sans mentir". Fair Use

8. Page 215 | "King of My Heart" Copyright © 2015 Meaux Jeaux Music (SESAC) Raucous Ruckus Publishing (SESAC) Sarah Mcmillan Publishing (SESAC) (adm. at CapitolCMGPublishing.com) All rights reserved. Used by permission.

9. Page 218 | "Captain" Copyright © 2015 Hillsong Music Publishing (APRA) (adm. in the US and Canada at CapitolCMGPublishing.com) All rights reserved. Used by permission.

10. Page 220 | Gone From My Sight: Also known as What Is Dying? By Rev. Luther F. Beecher, 1904 Public Domain

11. Page 223,224 | "Wonder." Oxford English and Spanish Dictionary. https://www.lexico.com/definition/wonder

12. Page 232 | "Like Thunder" written and performed by Brittany J Smith, Copyright 2020. Used by permission. All rights reserved.

13. Page 239 | "Purpose." Oxford English and Spanish Dictionary. https://www.lexico.com/definition/purpose

14. Page 258 | 1994. The Voyage of the Dawn Treader. New York: HarperCollinsPublishers. Lewis, C.S.

About the Author

Jacqueline (Jackie) Smith was born in Montevideo, Uruguay and moved to the United States as a little girl. Jackie and her husband David worked in children's ministry for almost 30 years. As children's pastors they spent those years traveling with their three children presenting family events throughout the United States and in missions to Central America. Together they designed and built creative ministry and entertainment experiences for churches, schools, and touring shows.

With years of curriculum and scriptwriting experience, Jackie has enjoyed being a speaker, business owner, themed party planner, wedding coordinator, and creative consultant. Jackie currently resides in Madison, Alabama where she enjoys a career in Real Estate. Jackie is available for speaking engagements to share her story and encourage others as they embark on their own Renaissance Belle.

You may contact Jackie at jsmith@renaissaincebelle.com
We invite you to visit www.renaissancebelle.com